BATTLE OF MIDWAY
AMERICA'S DECISIVE STRIKE IN THE PACIFIC IN WWII

BATTLE OF MIDWAY

AMERICA'S DECISIVE STRIKE IN THE PACIFIC IN WWII

John Grehan

BATTLE OF MIDWAY
America's Decisive Strike in the Pacific in WWII

First published in Great Britain in 2019 by Frontline Books,
an imprint of Pen & Sword Books Ltd,
Yorkshire – Philadelphia

Typeset in 9.5/12.5 Avenir by Dave Cassan. Printed and bound by CPI Group (UK) Ltd, Croydon CR0 4YY

Pen & Sword Books Ltd incorporates the imprints of Air World Books, Pen & Sword Archaeology, Atlas, Aviation, Battleground, Discovery, Family History, History, Maritime, Military, Naval, Politics, Social History, Transport, True Crime, Claymore Press, Frontline Books, Praetorian Press, Seaforth Publishing and White Owl

For a complete list of Pen & Sword titles please contact:

PEN & SWORD BOOKS LTD
47 Church Street, Barnsley, South Yorkshire, S70 2AS, UK.
E-mail: enquiries@pen-and-sword.co.uk
Website: www.pen-and-sword.co.uk

Or

PEN AND SWORD BOOKS,
1950 Lawrence Road, Havertown, PA 19083, USA
E-mail: Uspen-and-sword@casematepublishers.com
Website: www.penandswordbooks.com

CONTENTS

MAP LIST

ACKNOWLEDGEMENTS

The author and publisher would like to extend their grateful thanks, in no particular order, to the following individuals and organisations for their assistance with the images used in this publication: Robert Mitchell, James Luto, US Naval History and Heritage Command, US National Museum of Naval Aviation, US National Archives and Records Administration, National Museum of the US Air Force, United States Air Force, US Navy, US Library of Congress, US Army, and the US Air Force Historical Support Division.

The Build-up to Battle

By April 1942, Japan's strategy in its war against the Western Allies, principally Britain, Australia and the USA, had turned from committed offensive to defensive consolidation. Japan's tactics in pursuit of that strategy were, however, offensive in nature; Japan planned to seize additional outposts to guard the newly-gained Empire against attack and to cut enemy supply lines. The best form of defence, it was believed, was attack.

To a large degree, the Imperial Japanese forces had achieved all that had been expected in the early months – the First Phase – of the war. There remained just the campaigns in Burma and the Philippines to complete, and the capture of Port Moresby, the capital of Papua New Guinea, for Japan to have conquered the area it planned which would form the Greater East Asia Co-Prosperity Sphere.

The formation of this was to achieve a number of objectives. The first, and the openly-declared aim, was to create a self-sufficient 'bloc of Asian nations led by the Japanese and free of Western powers'. The undisclosed objectives were to secure the raw materials to keep Japan a modern industrial and military power, as well as establish a wide defensive ring around the home islands.

With the Philippines cut off from the USA, and the British forces in the region too weak to hold Burma, these ongoing campaigns were certain to end in victory for the Japanese. Nevertheless, Admiral Isoroku Yamamoto, commander-in-chief of the Japanese Combined Fleet and the man who had masterminded the raid on Pearl Harbor, knew that the US Pacific Fleet still remained a threat to Japan's ambitions, as he made clear to a gathering of fellow officers on board his flagship, *Yamato*, on 28 April 1942: 'The Second Phase Operations will be entirely different from the First Phase Operations. From now on, the enemy will be an alert and prepared enemy. The Combined Fleet cannot assume a long, drawn out defensive; on the contrary, we – the Navy – absolutely must take the offensive; we must strike the enemy with effective blows, hitting him where it hurts! The enemy's power is from 5 to 10 times ours; against this we must increase the intensity of our attacks, hitting the enemy's vital places, one after the other! … For these reasons, it is absolutely necessary that our naval air power overwhelms the enemy.'[1]

Yamamoto's wish for a decisive victory over the Pacific Fleet and the need perceived by others to create a defensive perimeter ultimately led to the battle that unfolded at Midway. This began with the Imperial General Headquarters agreeing to mount an operation to isolate Australia from the USA, by taking Port Moresby in Papua New Guinea, which was under Australian administration, as a prelude to the occupation of Tulagi, New Caledonia, Samoa and Fiji. It was believed, somewhat over-optimistically, that by cutting communications between Australia and America in this way, the former would surrender and submit to Imperial Japan.

Under the codename Operation *MO*, several powerful units of the Combined Fleet launched their attack against Port Moresby, the largest port in the South Pacific outside Australia, on 3-4 May 1942. But the Americans had intercepted and decoded Japanese signals, and sent two United States Navy carrier task forces and a joint Australian-US cruiser force, to oppose the Japanese move.

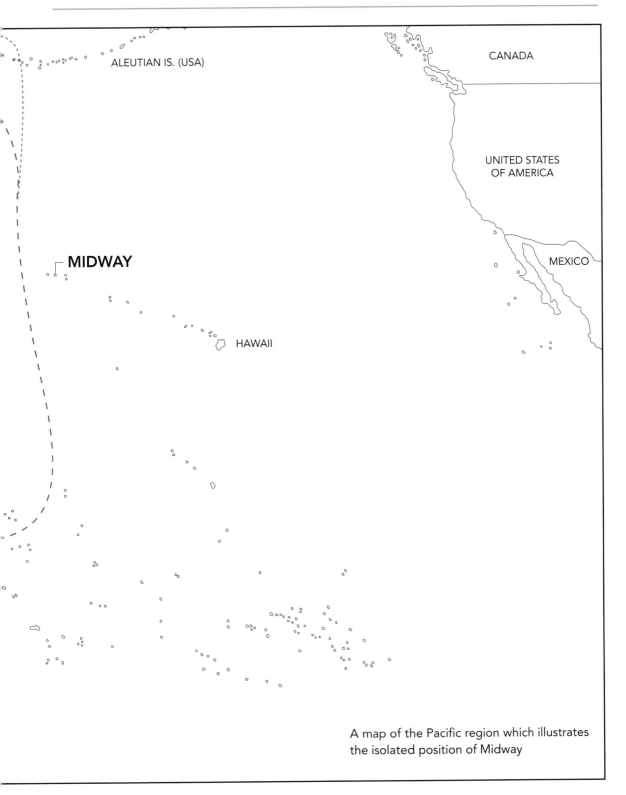

ALEUTIAN IS. (USA)

CANADA

UNITED STATES
OF AMERICA

MIDWAY

MEXICO

HAWAII

A map of the Pacific region which illustrates
the isolated position of Midway

The opposing forces clashed in the Coral Sea, midway between Australia and New Guinea. The battle was conducted solely by carrier-borne aircraft and was the first in history in which the vessels of neither side sighted or fired directly upon the other. Warfare was changing.

The Battle of the Coral Sea, resulted in the sinking of one carrier, USS *Lexington*, and serious damage to another, the USS *Yorktown*. In terms of material losses, the battle was considered a defeat for the US Navy. But the Japanese were forced to withdraw, and Port Moresby remained in Allied – more specifically Australian – hands. It was the first time in the war that a Japanese offensive had been stopped. The most significant consequence of the Battle of the Coral Sea was that one of Yamamoto's light carriers, *Shōhō*, was sunk and a fleet carrier, *Shōkaku*, was damaged and had to return to port for repairs, rendering it unavailable for the attack upon Midway. Significantly, *Shōhō* was the first Japanese aircraft carrier to be sunk in the Second World War.

Despite this setback to the Japanese, after Coral Sea, the Americans found themselves in a serious situation in the Pacific. It is true that a valuable base had been saved for the Allies, and there were indications that the Japanese had, temporarily at least, renounced any designs they might have had on isolating Australia. But the victory had been dearly bought.

The loss of one carrier and the damage to *Yorktown*, which was so severe as to require a considerable period of repair (estimated at two weeks), meant that the Americans found themselves outnumbered in the Pacific in terms of fleet aircraft carriers by two to one – all in a region where airpower had been clearly demonstrated to be of paramount importance. Of equal concern to the Americans was that the Battle of the Coral Sea had shown that their naval aircraft could not match those of the Japanese and that they lacked the screening forces to enable their battleships to be operated in support of the carriers. What better time could there be for the Imperial Japanese Navy to strike the US fleet and finish the job they started at Pearl Harbor?

That was the view of Admiral Yamamoto. The US Pacific Fleet's aircraft carriers had all been at sea when the Japanese attacked the Hawaiian base on 7 December 1941, which had meant the Americans still had a powerful offensive force. If, after the losses at Coral Sea, the remaining US carriers could be lured into a battle with the Combined Fleet and destroyed, nothing could stop the Japanese seizing control of the South Pacific.

It would take the United States many months, even with its massive industrial muscle, to rebuild its carrier fleet if it was destroyed, by which time Japan would be able to secure the raw materials needed to keep its war machine functioning and to build all the bases it required across the Pacific, which would enable its aircraft to dominate the land and the seas.

The US Navy, well aware of its weaknesses, would be very wary of allowing its carriers to be drawn into a battle it had not initiated. Only the severest threat would induce Admiral Chester William Nimitz, Commander-in-Chief Pacific Ocean Areas, to commit his carriers to action. Yamamoto, therefore, devised a complex plan which, he believed, would persuade Nimitz to throw caution to the wind and release his carriers, by attacking another US base in the Hawaiian Islands – the US Naval Air Station on the Midway Atoll which is near the north-western end of the Hawaiian archipelago. Yamamoto would then pounce on the US carriers with his powerful battleships and, at a stroke, end any hope the Americans might have of winning the war in the Pacific.

Japanese intelligence of the disposition of the American carriers, though, was far from complete. They knew of the presence of the USS *Enterprise* and USS *Hornet* in the Pacific and placed them in the Hawaiian area. They believed *Ranger* was in the Atlantic but could get no reliable information as to the whereabouts of *Wasp*. Some of the American prisoners taken in the Battle of the Coral Sea stated that the USS *Lexington* had been sunk, though others claimed that she was under repair on the west coast of the United States – the former was in fact the case. The two or three American auxiliary (escort) carriers which were placed in the Pacific were known to be slow and were not considered by the Japanese to be capable of effective employment in offensive operations. The Japanese did not expect that the Americans had any powerful unit, built round aircraft carriers, in the neighbourhood of Midway.

A sortie by the American naval forces in the Hawaii area, in the event of an attack on Midway, was of course expected. The strength of these forces was estimated as follows:

Aircraft carriers	2-3
Escort carriers	2-3
Battleships	2
Cruisers	7-9
Light cruisers	4
Destroyers	About 30
Submarines	25

Yamamoto felt that he could easily defeat this, or any other force, even if the Americans were supported by the Royal Navy. The Japanese were also aware that after Coral Sea, the US had reinforced its air strength at Midway, which now amounted to two squadrons of Consolidated PBY Catalina reconnaissance flying boats plus one squadron of bombers and one of fighters.

They believed that strict air patrols were maintained both day and night to a distance of about 500 to 600 miles from Midway and that approximately three fighters were kept over the islands at all times. Air reconnaissance, it was understood, was conducted mainly to the west and to the south, and less thorough to the north-west and north. It was also thought that patrols by surface vessels were maintained, with submarine patrols to the west.

Air strength in the Hawaii area, which could be used for the speedy reinforcement of Midway, was estimated at about sixty flying boats, 100 bombers and some 200 fighters. It was considered that the Japanese combat air patrols from their carriers plus the warships' anti-aircraft fire could deal successfully with any attempt to counter-attack by US shore-based aircraft – whether it was from Midway or Hawaii. It was also fully acknowledged that Midway was very strongly defended, with powerful fixed fortifications, high-angle guns and a garrison of marines, but the invasion force would be of sufficient strength to overcome the island's defences.

The Midway Atoll is composed of three islands – Sand Island, Eastern Island and the tiny Spit Island – and landings would be made on all three. Despite the strength of the US base, the islands are very small and it was felt that no more than six transports would be needed to convey the naval landing force, consisting of some 1,500 marines to take Sand Island and 1,000 Army troops for Eastern Island, together with engineers and ancillary units, totalling some 5,000 men. After what was expected to be the quick capture of the islands, two construction battalions would put the base into defensible condition. To accomplish this before the anticipated clash with the US fleet, the men were given just one day, although it was expected that it would take three days for the Pacific Fleet to respond, by which time the island would be turned into a fortress, with the fighters from the carriers defending the skies above and midget torpedoes and motor torpedo boats protecting the coastline.[2]

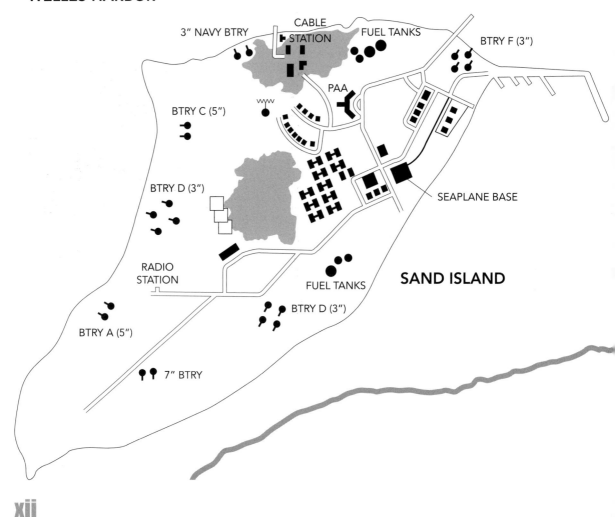

MIDWAY ISLANDS

JUNE 1942

- Gun 3" or larger
- Command Post
- Radar
- Overgrown area

BTRY Battery

0 SCALE - YARDS 1,000

LAGOON

WELLES HARBOR

3" NAVY BTRY
CABLE STATION
FUEL TANKS
BTRY F (3")
PAA
BTRY C (5")
BTRY D (3")
SEAPLANE BASE
RADIO STATION
FUEL TANKS
SAND ISLAND
BTRY D (3")
BTRY A (5")
7" BTRY

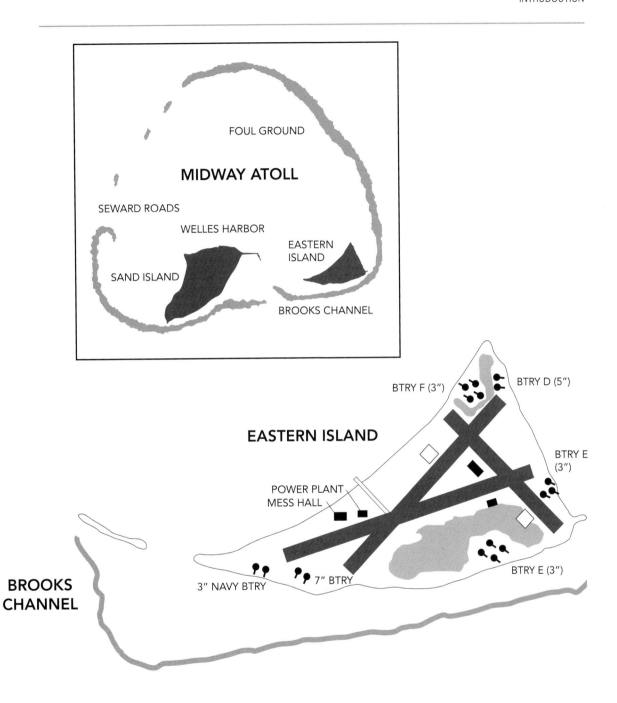

FOUL GROUND

MIDWAY ATOLL

SEWARD ROADS

WELLES HARBOR

EASTERN ISLAND

SAND ISLAND

BROOKS CHANNEL

BTRY F (3")

BTRY D (5")

EASTERN ISLAND

BTRY E (3")

POWER PLANT
MESS HALL

3" NAVY BTRY

7" BTRY

BTRY E (3")

BROOKS CHANNEL

PACIFIC OCEAN

Two seaplane carriers were to convey the 11th Air Flotilla which was to establish a seaplane base on Curé Island, some fifty-six miles to the west of Midway. The escort for this transport unit was to be carried out by the 2nd Destroyer Flotilla, consisting of the light cruiser *Jintsu*, flagship of Rear-Admiral R. Tanaka, who commanded the unit and its close escort, and eleven destroyers. The only apparent drawback was that the assault forces were ill-supplied with landing boats. They carried many different kinds of craft but were far from confident that all of them could cross the reefs, in which case rubber boats were supposed to be used.

Yamamoto, however, would not be able to deploy his full strength for the operation because of opposition from the Imperial Japanese Army (IJA). The Army's General Staff wanted to occupy the western Aleutian Islands to place the Japanese home islands out of range of US bombers based at airfields in Alaska. In order to get the assistance he wanted from the Army for the invasion of Midway, Yamamoto had to agree to providing support for the capture of the Aleutians at the approximate same date as the operation against Midway. This entailed providing air cover, in the form of two light carriers, as well as five cruisers, twelve destroyers, six submarines, and four troop transports, along with supporting auxiliary ships. The desire by the IJA to establish a protective ring around the home islands had already led to the sinking of one of Yamamoto's carriers at the Coral Sea and the operational loss of three others. The presence of these ships would, most likely, have changed the course of the Battle of Midway.

In what was codenamed Operation *MI*, Yamamoto divided his remaining force into three groups. The first of these was the Midway Occupation Force, cover for which was provided by the 2nd Fleet, formed at this point by part of the 3rd Battle Squadron, led by Vice Admiral Kondo, Commander-in-Chief of the Occupation Force, in the battleship *Kongō*, plus the battleship *Hiei*, the 4th Cruiser Squadron (*Atago* and *Mava*), 5th Cruiser Squadron (*Myoko* and *Haguro*) and the 4th Destroyer Flotilla, led by the light cruiser *Yura* with seven destroyers. The four cruisers of the 7th Cruiser Squadron (*Kumano*, flagship of Rear Admiral T. Kurita, with *Suzuya*, *Mikuma* and *Mogami*) constituted a fast support force which was to take up a position between 75 and 100 miles ahead of the transports during the approach to Midway. It was intended that this force should shell Midway prior to the landing.

The second group, the Carrier Striking Force of the 1st Air Fleet (the *Kidō Butai* or 'Mobile Force'), with the carriers *Akagi*, *Raga*, *Hiryu* and *Soryu* and commanded by Admiral C. Nagumo, had the dual role of attacking the US Fleet if located, and supporting the invasion force. The carriers were supported by the 2nd Division of the 3rd Battle Squadron (the battleships *Haruna* and *Kirishima*), the 8th Cruiser Squadron (*Tone* and *Chikuma*), and the 10th Destroyer Flotilla (light cruiser *Nagara* and sixteen destroyers).

Yamamoto's First Fleet Main Force, the one that he hoped would finally crush the Pacific Fleet, led by him in person, consisted of the 1st and 2nd Battle Squadrons, totalling seven battleships, two cruisers of the 9th Cruiser Squadron, the 3rd Destroyer Flotilla (the cruiser *Sendai* and twelve destroyers), and the light cruiser *Zuiho*.

Though the Combined Fleet still possessed greater material strength than the US Navy's Pacific Fleet in terms of aircraft carriers and battleships, the intense and almost constant operations, which had lasted for more than five months, had seen a considerable turn-over in aircrew personnel, and there was time for no more than basic training for most of the newly-recruited airmen. Only one carrier was available for take-off and landing drills and the inexperienced flyers barely reached the point where they could make daytime landings on carriers, and only the more experienced pilots carried out about one dusk landing apiece.

There were no opportunities for bomber leaders to participate in formation bombing drills. The only target ship, the old battleship *Settsu*, was limited to waters in the western Inland Sea, with the resultant loss of valuable time flying to and from there, reducing the period which could be devoted to bombing drills. Even this minimum practice could not be conducted satisfactorily since the men were kept busy with maintenance work. In air combat tactics only the more experienced got further than lone air combat exercise and even they were limited to about a three-plane formation. But Japan had only planned for a short war and had hoped that by the summer of 1942 they would be facing the Americans over the negotiating table not over the barrel of a gun or an aircraft's bomb-sight.

Based in Hawaii, Station Hypo, also known as Fleet Radio Unit Pacific, had been intercepting Japanese naval signals regarding a strike against a target referred to as 'AF' as early as March 1942 and against the Aleutians a month later. Beginning on 1 May, Japanese Navy communications activity from the vicinity of Japan began to increase noticeably. Navy analysts soon realized that the additional intercepts reflected naval exercises conducted in preparation for both operations. Though it was suspected that 'AF' was Midway, this remained unconfirmed – until Hypo's Captain Wilfred J. 'Jasper' Holmes came up with a brilliant idea.

Knowing that Midway depended on desalinated water, Holmes used an old undersea cable to send a message to the military there. He asked them to send out an un-coded radio message stating that the purification system had broken down: 'We have only enough water for two weeks. Please supply us immediately.'[3] A few days later, the code breakers picked up a Japanese message saying that AF had water problems. That made it certain. They now knew that the Japanese would send a small force to the Aleutian Islands, as originally planned, but that the main target would be Midway.

By studying the form and the substance of the intercepted communications, US Navy analysts obtained an abundance of detail about the Japanese plans and the magnitude of the forces to be arrayed against each objective. Over the course of the following weeks, more information was gathered, enabling Nimitz, and Admiral Ernest J. King, Chief of Naval Operations, to understand Yamamoto's intentions.

The two formations Nimitz intended to employ at Midway, Task Forces 16 and 17, made rendezvous at 15.30 hours on 2 June, about 350 miles north-east of Midway, having fuelled at sea en route. The combined force, under the command of Rear Admiral Fletcher, moved to the area of operations north of Midway, Task Force 17 operating about ten miles to the southward of Task Force 16.

Task Force 17 contained just the single carrier USS *Yorktown*, two heavy cruisers, and five destroyers. The *Yorktown*'s aircraft were bolstered by the addition of squadrons from the USS *Saratoga*, to a total of thirty-six scout bombers, twelve torpedo bombers, and twenty-five fighters. The *Enterprise* and *Hornet* in Task Force 16 each carried thirty-five scout bombers, fourteen torpedo bombers, and twenty-seven fighters. The lesson of the Battle of the Coral Sea, when the American fighters were outnumbered at every encounter, had resulted in a 50 per cent increase in the number of fighters borne, bringing them to numerical equality with the Japanese, ship for ship.

As Nimitz had correctly assumed that the reason for Yamamoto's attack upon Midway was to ensnare the Pacific Fleet, he told Rear Admiral Frank Jack Fletcher that his actions should 'be governed by the principle of calculated risk which you shall interpret to mean the avoidance of exposure of your forces to attack by superior enemy forces without good prospect of inflicting, as a result of such exposure, greater damage to the enemy'.

A multi-layered submarine cordon was established to cover the approaches to Midway, with three submarines patrolling in a circle 200 miles from the atoll and six submarines in a circle 150 miles distant. Two other submarines, the USS *Flying Fish* and USS *Cachalot*, were placed on station patrols some sixty miles north-north-west and north-west of Midway respectively, and USS *Cuttlefish* 700 miles to the west. Three more were placed in support 800 miles north-west of Pearl Harbor and four 300 miles north of the Pacific Fleet's main base. Altogether, nineteen of the US Navy's twenty-six submarines in the Pacific, all the ones that could reach the area in time, were to be employed in this operation.

The Carrier Striking Force, *Kidō Butai*, sailed from Hashira Jima at 09.00 hours on 26 May 1942. The ships refuelled at sea on 31 May and 1 June. Visibility steadily decreased from about 13.00 hours on 1 June, resulting in refuelling being discontinued before all the ships had been serviced. By 14.00 hours that day, the carrier force was completely enveloped in fog. By the morning of 3 June, surface visibility had improved greatly, though there were still scattered clouds above.

Yamamoto's Main Force was around thirty hours behind the *Kidō Butai*, but took a shorter route to the area of operations. At 15.00 hours on 3 June, Yamamoto detached a screening force to the northwards to protect the main force. It played no further part in the campaign, only re-joining the main force after the battle.

The 2nd Fleet, which was to provide distant cover for the Occupation Force, sailed with the Main Force, sailing south-westwards until it rendezvoused with the troop transport unit with its close escort which had sailed earlier from the Inland Sea. It had been serviced at Saipan, from where it sailed at 21.00 hours on 27 May with the intention of assaulting Midway from the south. Passing west of Tinian, it picked up some of the slowest transports which had sailed from Eniwetok, the westernmost of the Marshall Islands, and proceeded towards the rendezvous with the Second Fleet. Air cover was provided by the 24th Air Flotilla from the Marshall Islands and the 26th from Marcus Island.

Measures were taken to strengthen Midway to the maximum extent possible. The problem at Midway for the Americans was to hit the enemy before they were hit. The danger against which they had to guard was that their aircraft might be surprised on the ground and destroyed, and their runways put temporarily out of action by bombing, before the enemy was damaged. There were two essential requirements to prevent this – effective search and long-range striking power.

For long-range search, thirty US Navy Catalinas were despatched to the island, and for long-range strikes seventeen Boeing B-17s of the Seventh Air Force and four USAAF Martin B-26 Marauders, fitted with torpedoes, were sent to Midway from Hawaii, in spite of the difficulty of protecting these aircraft on the ground.

Major General C.L. Tinker, Commander of the USAAF in Hawaii, travelled to Midway to assess the situation for himself. As a result, to provide close-in air striking power, the Marine air group was brought up to a strength of twenty-eight fighters and thirty-four scout bombers, though only thirty pilots were available for the latter. This group was augmented by six new Navy torpedo bombers. Because of overcrowding of the facilities at Midway there was considerable interchange between that island and Hawaii, so that the number of aircraft available varied from day to day. The figures stated here are those for 3 June, the day before the battle. The radio and communication facilities on Midway were reinforced to enable the handling of all these extra aircraft.

While all the Army and Navy aircraft sent to Midway were under the control of Captain Cyril T. Simard, the Commanding Officer Naval Air Station Midway, there was no coordination between the carrier task forces and Midway. This was to ensure that the Japanese had no inkling of the approach or whereabouts of the US ships, which also were to sail under conditions of complete radio silence.

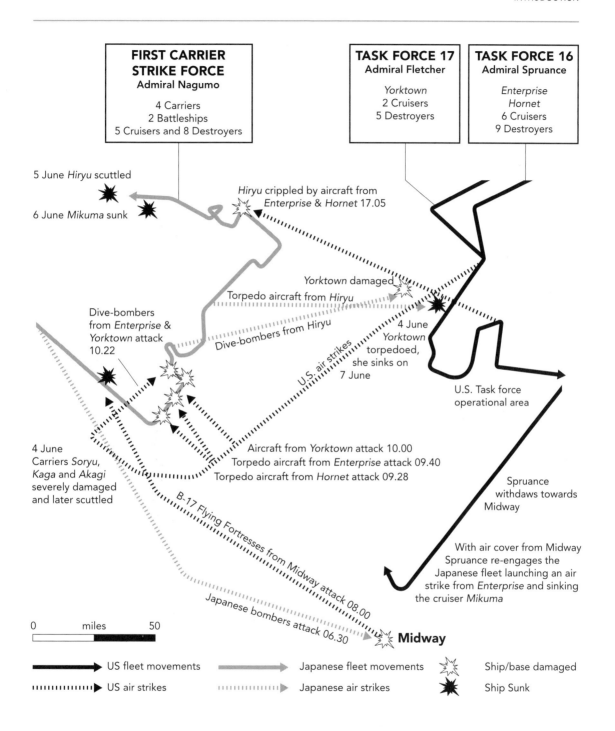

FIRST CARRIER STRIKE FORCE
Admiral Nagumo

4 Carriers
2 Battleships
5 Cruisers and 8 Destroyers

TASK FORCE 17
Admiral Fletcher

Yorktown
2 Cruisers
5 Destroyers

TASK FORCE 16
Admiral Spruance

Enterprise
Hornet
6 Cruisers
9 Destroyers

5 June *Hiryu* scuttled

6 June *Mikuma* sunk

Hiryu crippled by aircraft from *Enterprise* & *Hornet* 17.05

Yorktown damaged

Torpedo aircraft from *Hiryu*

Dive-bombers from *Enterprise* & *Yorktown* attack 10.22

Dive-bombers from *Hiryu*

U.S. air strikes

4 June *Yorktown* torpedoed, she sinks on 7 June

U.S. Task force operational area

4 June Carriers *Soryu*, *Kaga* and *Akagi* severely damaged and later scuttled

Aircraft from *Yorktown* attack 10.00
Torpedo aircraft from *Enterprise* attack 09.40
Torpedo aircraft from *Hornet* attack 09.28

Spruance withdaws towards Midway

With air cover from Midway Spruance re-engages the Japanese fleet launching an air strike from *Enterprise* and sinking the cruiser *Mikuma*

B-17 Flying Fortresses from Midway attack 08.00

Japanese bombers attack 06.30 **Midway**

0 miles 50

→ US fleet movements
→ Japanese fleet movements
✺ Ship/base damaged

▸ US air strikes
▹ Japanese air strikes
✸ Ship Sunk

The Battle of Midway

In the belief that the Japanese planned a rendezvous about 700 miles west of Midway, B-17s undertook searches to a distance of 800 miles on 31 May and 1 June, and on 2 June a B-17 without bombs searched 800 miles to the west without making contact with the enemy. The skies were clear that day, except beyond 300 miles to the north and north-west where visibility was poor – and it was precisely this area of low visibility and fog that concealed the approaching Japanese carrier force for some thirty hours until it came within 650 miles of Midway.

Of course, the possibility that the Japanese strike force was making good use of these conditions to approach Midway was not discounted. But the poor weather was almost certain to mean that no attack would be attempted as navigation and bombing accuracy would be compromised, and it precluded any night attack. It was thought that as the Japanese moved out of the cover of the bad weather to launch their attack, they would do so at dawn. This would be between 04.30 hours and 05.00 hours, resulting in the enemy aircraft reaching Midway around 06.00 hours.

To counter the threat of a dawn attack, search aircraft were sent off as early as possible each day, usually about 04.15 hours. To safeguard them from destruction, and to ensure that a striking force would be available immediately if a target was located, the B-17s took off directly afterwards. They remained in the air for about four hours, by which time the progress of the search and the reduction of their fuel load rendered landing possible. The other aircraft remained on the ground but fully alert until the search had reached a distance of 400 miles without detecting an enemy presence.

The garrison of Midway was increased to the maximum. The US Marine's Sixth Defence Battalion was reinforced by part of the Second Raider Battalion, with special equipment for opposing a mechanised landing, and by the Anti-Aircraft and Special Weapons Group of the Third Defence Battalion. The troops worked day and night to strengthen the defences of the islands. Underwater obstacles were installed, and anti-tank and anti-personnel mines planted. Motor Torpedo Boat Squadron One was also sent from Hawaii to help provide inshore defence as well as assisting in the rescue of downed aircrew.

Yamamoto thought that he would have three days to take and secure Midway before the Pacific Fleet arrived. But the American aircraft carriers were already lying in wait. The opening shots of what would prove to be the most decisive battle of the war in the Pacific were about to be fired.

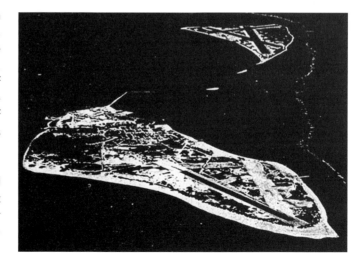

Opposite: The US Naval Air Station at Midway. An aerial photograph, looking just south of west across the southern side of Midway atoll. Eastern Island, then the site of Midway's airfield, is in the foreground. Sand Island, location of most other base facilities, is across the entrance channel. (NARA)

Right: A poor-quality image of Sand Island and Eastern Island (furthest from the camera) taken in 1942 for a Japanese Intelligence Brief on Midway.

Above: An Imperial Japanese Navy photograph of Admiral Isoroku Yamamoto when he was Commander-in-Chief, Combined Fleet. (USNHHC)

Above: Vice Admiral Frank Jack Fletcher, the commander of US Task Force 17, photographed on 17 September 1942. (NARA)

Above: A photograph of the Carrier Striking Force in the spring of 1942.·

Opposite page top: Preparing for battle. Arriving at Pearl Harbor with Task Force 17 on 27 May 1942, following the Battle of Coral Sea, is the heavy cruiser USS *Astoria* (CA-34). Her crew is in whites, paraded at quarters on the forecastle, and a motor launch is being lowered by her port boat crane. (NARA)

Opposite page bottom: Also shown at Pearl Harbor just before sailing for Midway is the Porter-class destroyer USS *Phelps* which was part of Task Force 16. (NARA)

Right: Vice Admiral Chuichi Nagumo. An Imperial Japanese Navy portrait of Chuichi Nagumo in 1942 as commander of the Carrier Striking Force. (USNHHC)

Above: The battleship *Yamato*. After the destruction of most of the US Pacific Fleet's battleships, the Imperial Japanese Navy possessed the strongest surface fleet in the region, which included the flagship of the Combined Force, the battleship *Yamato* which, along with her sister ship, *Musashi,* were the heaviest and most powerfully armed battleships ever constructed, displacing 72,800 tonnes at full load and armed with nine 18.1-inch guns. The design of these two battleships contravened the terms of the Washington Naval Treaty which limited capital ships to a displacement of 35,000 tons and guns of no greater calibre than 16-inches. *Yamato* is shown here on 20 October 1941. (USNHHC)

Right: Colonel Harold D. Shannon, USMC, the man placed in command of Midway's Marine Sixth Defense Battalion. (NARA)

Below: Admiral Chester W. Nimitz is seen here presenting awards to naval personnel on the flight deck of the carrier USS *Enterprise* at Pearl Harbor on 27 May 1942. As Nimitz pinned the Distinguished Flying Cross on Lieutenant Roger W. Mehle for actions in a raid against the Marshall Islands on 1 February 1942, he told the young aviator, 'I think you'll have a chance to win yourself another medal in the next several days'. Nimitz, of course, was speaking of the upcoming Battle of Midway. In fact, that very day, Nimitz promulgated Operation Plan 29-42, which outlined his plan to ensnare Yamamoto's Striking Force. As it happened, Lieutenant Mehle would find himself leading a section of Grumman F4F Wildcats of Fighting Squadron (VF) 6 defending USS *Yorktown* on 4 June, only to have his guns malfunction. (US National Naval Aviation Museum)

Above: The US base at Midway was no stranger to Japanese attack. The first enemy strike occurred on 7 December 1941, the same day as the infamous attack on Pearl Harbor, when the atoll was bombarded by the destroyers *Ushio* and *Sazanami*, both of which had been part of the Japanese fleet at Pearl Harbor. The engagement began at 09.31 hours and lasted fifty-four minutes.

As one account notes, 'the American command, communications and power plant building was damaged by a 5 in (130 mm) shell, which deflected off an adjacent laundromat.

Battery "H" commander – First Lieutenant George H. Cannon – was hit by shrapnel in the pelvis while inside the command building. By this time, the communications were down from enemy fire, so Lieutenant Cannon refused medical attention until he was assured that the communications were restored to the post and the wounded marines around him were evacuated. By the time Cannon received aid from a medic, it was too late; he perished due to blood loss. For Cannon's "distinguished conduct in the line of his profession, extraordinary courage, and disregard of his own condition", he received the first Medal of Honor issued to a US Marine for actions in the Second World War.' A

street on Sand Island was named after Cannon and continues to be known by that name.

It is also worth noting that the facilities at Midway were also bombarded by a Japanese submarine in February 1942.

This picture shows one of the attackers, the Imperial Japanese Navy's destroyer *Sazanami*, the second Japanese warship to bear that name, pictured on 15 April 1940. Launched in 1931, *Sazanami* was sunk by the submarine USS *Albacore* on 12 January 1944. (Kure Maritime Museum)

Opposite page top: The aftermath of the bombardment by the Japanese destroyers *Ushio* and *Sazanami* on 7 December 1941 – the fire-gutted bow section of a PBY-3 Catalina hit by one of the shells fired. (USNHHC)

Opposite page bottom: The laundry building on Sand Island (in the foreground in this view), was damaged during the night raid carried out by Japanese destroyers *Ushio* and *Sazanami* on 7 December 1941. This view was taken looking southwest along Sand Island's southern side. This building was hit again, by Japanese air attack, on 4 June 1942, during the Battle of Midway - see page 28. (USNHHC)

Above: Second Lieutenant Francis P. McCarthy USMCR, of Marine Fighting Squadron 221 (VMF-221), can be seen on the left being congratulated by Admiral Chester W. Nimitz, Commander-in-Chief, Pacific, after he was presented with the Distinguished Flying Cross for his part in shooting down a Japanese Kawanishi H8K flying boat, which had been gathering intelligence, near Midway on 10 March 1942. The ceremony for the presentation of McCarthy's DFC took place on Midway on 2 May 1942. As we shall see, VMF-221 played an important part in the fighting in June that year. (USNHHC)

Chapter 1

FIRST CONTACT

3 June 1942

04.07 hours   **Attack on Dutch Harbor**

The opening round of the Midway campaign began, in effect, with the attack on the US Navy's Dutch Harbor Naval Operating Base in the Aleutian Islands of Alaska. Early commentators believed that the Japanese assault upon the Aleutians was intended to act as a diversion to distract the attention of the Pacific Fleet away from Midway. Later, it was found that these were two separate operations, though inevitably linked and generally regarded as part of the Midway campaign as a whole. In this image we can see US Marines observing the attack upon Dutch Harbor from their trenches. (Department of the Navy, Naval Photographic Center)

Right: This A6M2 Zero, trailing smoke and probably damaged, was photographed during the attacks on Dutch Harbor. (USNHHC)

Below: A Mitsubishi A6M2 Zero pictured on the quayside at Dutch Harbor, Alaska, on 17 July 1942. This aircraft, from carrier *Ryujo*, had crash landed after the Dutch Harbor Raid on 4 June 1942. Salvaged by VP-41, it was the first Zero captured intact for flight tests. (USNHHC)

Opposite page:

09.04 hours   **First Sighting**

It was on 3 June, that the Japanese ships which constituted part of the Midway Occupation Force were first sighted. That morning the aircraft from Midway had set off for their usual search areas, and by 04.30 hours all aircraft fit for service were in the air, in order to clear the runways. As on previous days, the Catalinas flew 700 miles to the north-west. Visibility was good apart from the area of bad weather to the north-north-west which was by then 400 miles out from Midway.

A few hours later reports began to be received at Midway, from the Catalinas, indicating the approach of an enemy surface fleet. It was the ships carrying the Occupation Force. First contact with the transport ships was made at 09.04 hours; the Catalina crew involved reported seeing two large cargo ships, but these were in fact minesweepers.

This representation by Norman Bel Geddes depicts the sighting of the Japanese minesweepers *Tama Maru No.3* and *Tama Maru No.5* by the Midway-based Patrol Squadron 23 (VP-23) Catalina flown by Ensign James P.O. Lyle, at 09.04 hours on 3 June 1942. These two Japanese vessels had left Wake on 31 May. (USNHHC)

09.24 hours   **A Further Sighting**

Below: Twenty minutes after Ensign Lyle's crew spotted the two minesweepers, at 09.24 hours Ensign Jack Reid, flying a Catalina from Patrol Squadron 44 (VP-44), sighted a larger group of Japanese ships. His crew, patrolling to the west of Lyle's, immediately transmitted the discovery back to Midway with the words 'Main Body'. A few moments later, Reid reported that the distance from Midway was 700 miles and that the ships, steaming at ten knots, had a bearing of 262 degrees. At 09.50 hours, Reid also reported that the force consisted of eleven vessels.[4]

Several smaller groups of ships were reported about the same time and were correctly interpreted as also belonging to the Occupation Force and its escort, which were all converging on a rendezvous for the final advance on Midway.

This painting by John Hamilton depicts Reid's PBY Catalina circling the Japanese vessels after they were spotted by his crew. (USNHHC)

Opposite page top: The crew of Ensign Jack Reid's PBY-5A Catalina of Patrol Squadron 44 (VP-44) that sighted the approaching Japanese fleet's Midway Occupation Force on the morning of 3 June 1942. Standing left to right are: Aviation Machinist's Mate 2nd Class R.J. Derouin; Chief Aviation Radioman Francis Musser; Ensign Hardeman (co-pilot); Ensign J.H. Reid (pilot), on the wheel; and Ensign R.A. Swan (navigator). Kneeling in front, left to right, are: Aviation Machinist's Mate 1st Class J.F. Gammell (naval aviation pilot); Aviation Machinist's Mate 3rd Class J. Goovers; Aviation Machinist's Mate 3rd Class P.A. Fitzpatrick. (USNHHC)

Opposite page bottom: It was not until 11.00 hours on 3 June 1942, that Midway's Air

Commander, Captain Logan C. Ramsey USN, realised that the 'Main Body' spotted by Ensign Reid's Catalina was in fact the Midway Occupation Force and not the main Japanese carrier force. That said, the sighting of these eleven vessels just 700 miles from Midway gave the first clear indication that Station Hypo had correctly interpreted the enemy's intentions and that Midway was the prime target of the impending attack.[5] Word of the sighting of the Japanese warships quickly spread through the US forces in the area.

This picture of Captain Logan C. Ramsey USN was taken on 8 March 1943. At the time he was speaking to mark his taking command of the Bogue-class escort carrier USS *Block Island* at the Puget Sound Navy Yard. (USNHHC)

**12.30 hours   B-17 Strike Force Takes-off
                                    From Midway**

Above: Ensign Reid's Catalina was ordered to return to base on account of being low on fuel and the probability of it being shot down if it attempted to shadow the enemy force. At 11.58 hours, Captain Simard, the Naval Commander at Midway, ordered that a single B-17 be equipped with extra supplies of fuel and then head out to re-establish contact with, and track, the Japanese ships. The B-17 also carried no bombs but it did have a Navy observer onboard to relay information about the Japanese force – still reported to be about 600 to 700 miles south-west of Midway.

As none of the sightings had made any specific mention of seeing the Japanese aircraft carriers, Captain Simard was unwilling to commit the rest of his long-range B-17 bombers until he was certain that the Carrier Striking Force was present. But a little after midday, further reports were received that a large enemy force consisting of two or three heavy cruisers and about thirty other ships, including destroyers, transports, and cargo vessels, had reached Midway.

Though the carriers had still not been found, this was enough for the commanding officer at Midway. Consequently, very shortly after the solo B-17 had taken to the sky, a

strike force of B-17s of the Seventh Air Force was dispatched.

In the photograph on the opposite page are shown the US Army Air Force B-17E Flying Fortress bombers which took off from the airfield on Eastern Island, Midway Atoll, to attack the Japanese invasion fleet. (USNHHC)

16.23 hours   The B-17s Strike

The force of B-17s from Midway, which was led by Lieutenant Colonel Walter C. Sweeney USAAC, located the Japanese ships at 16.23 hours at a distance from Midway of about 570 miles.

The attack was made in three flights of three planes each at 8,000, 10,000, and 12,000 feet respectively.

Anti-aircraft fire was so heavy that it was considered unwise to stay to observe results. However, a heavy cruiser and a transport were claimed to have been hit, along with a second cruiser that was believed to be have been hit at the stern. Subsequent research revealed that none of the Japanese vessels suffered a direct hit.

The lone B-17 sent out by Captain Simard never found the enemy ships and duly returned to Midway. By 21.45 hours, all of the bombers had returned to base. Shown above is a Boeing B-17B at Pearl Harbor. (US Air Force)

21.15 hours   Catalinas Follow up the B-17s

At 21.15 hours, four PBY-5As (three of which had flown to Midway from Pearl Harbor, a ten-hour flight, that afternoon), took off on an historic sortie, each carrying a single Mk.XIII Mod. I torpedo. The pilots, led by Lieutenant William L. Richards, Executive Officer of Patrol Squadron 44 (VP-44), were all volunteers. Their orders were simple: locate the enemy and attack with torpedoes. They subsequently undertook what was the first ever night torpedo attack by US patrol aircraft on surface ships. This photograph shows a Consolidated PBY-5A Catalina patrol bomber dropping a Mk.XIII torpedo. (USNHHC)

Above: Though the weather was clear, the last two Catalinas lost contact with the leading pair when passing through cloud. The Japanese ships were found at around 01.15 hours on the 4th about 500 miles from Midway. The two Catalinas approached without lights, the leader dropping his torpedo at 100 feet, aiming at the largest of the ships approximately 800 yards distant. The second aircraft dropped its torpedo just 200 yards from the target and opened machine-gun fire on the ship. It was reported that one of the torpedoes may have struck a ship. The Catalinas were ordered to return to Laysan Island to avoid being caught up in the predicted Japanese attack on Midway.

The third of the planes, piloted by Ensign Gaylord D. Propst, which had lost touch with the two leading Catalinas, found the Japanese fleet independently and also attacked and believed that he saw the flash of an explosion. Propst was chased by a Japanese fighter but managed to escape through cloud.

The other Catalina which lost its way ran out of fuel and landed on the sea near Lisianski Island. The crew was rescued fifty-three hours later.

Shown here are the pilots of the four Catalinas from Patrol Squadron 24 (VP-24) and Patrol Squadron 51 (VP-51) that flew the torpedo attack mission. From left to right they are: Lieutenant (Junior Grade) Douglas C. Davis of VP-24; Ensign Allan Rothenberg of VP-51; Lieutenant William L. Richards, Executive Officer of Patrol Squadron 44 (VP-44), who flew in a VP-24 aircraft on this mission; and Ensign Gaylord D. Propst of VP-24. (NARA)

Chapter 2

BOMBS FALL ON MIDWAY

4 June 1942

04.15 hours   **The Hunt for the Enemy Carriers**

A number of Catalinas took off from Midway at 04.15 hours in the hope of spotting the hitherto undetected Japanese carriers. There were four squadrons of Catalinas on Midway with a total of thirty-one aircraft. Protected by a Marine fighter patrol they were ordered to search up to 425 miles from Midway and then land at the Hawaiian Islands of Laysan and Lisianski as it was thought that their base would be under attack and would be too hazardous for them to return.

Following the Catalinas into the air from Midway were the B-17s of the 72nd Squadron, 5th Bomb Group. In as much as they would have to remain in the air for at least four hours under any circumstances, they were ordered to attack the ships of the Occupation Force to the west, which, it was estimated, were to be found at a distance of about 480 miles. They were warned, however, to expect a change of orders if the enemy carriers should be discovered in the meantime.

This image shows maintenance work being undertaken on a PBY-5A Catalina in 1942. (USNHHC)

Above: A typical scene for those at sea early in the morning of 4 June 1942. A junior officer poses with a 20mm gun on USS *Yorktown*, waiting for the action to begin. This gun is one of five in *Yorktown*'s after port 20mm battery. (NARA)

Opposite page: The waiting game continues.

Two crewmen pass the time with a round of 'acey-deucey', a simple board game that is a variant of backgammon, on board USS *Yorktown* during the morning of 4 June 1942. They are playing on the working platform of one of the ship's eight 5/38 dual-purpose guns before the battle. (USNHHC)

04.30 hours   **The Japanese Raiders Take Off**

At 04.30 hours on 4 June, Admiral Nagumo, flying his flag in the carrier *Akagi*, launched his initial attack on Midway, the intention being to neutralise the island's defences prior to the landing of the Occupation Force. He was completely unaware that the US carrier fleet was in the vicinity. This view of *Akagi* with B5N torpedo bombers arranged on its flight deck was taken on 26 March 1942. (Maritime History and Science Museum, Kure)

Above: There was a south-easterly breeze and a calm sea as *Akagi*'s crew prepared the attacking aircraft, making for ideal launching conditions. This first assault force consisted of thirty-six Aichi D3A Type 99 dive bombers and thirty-six Nakajima B5N 'Kate' torpedo bombers, escorted by thirty-six Mitsubishi A6M Zero fighters. In accordance with Japanese protocol, this total of 108 aircraft was exactly half of Nagumo's strike force, the other half being kept in hand to be deployed as circumstances dictated. The other 108 aircraft – eighteen dive bombers each from *Hiryu* and *Soryu* and eighteen torpedo bombers from *Akagi* and *Kaga*, as well as thirty-six fighters – were brought up from the hangars after the first wave had departed and began preparing on the flight decks of the carriers. With seventy-two Zeros either in the first wave or being held in readiness with the second wave, only eighteen fighters were available to provide immediate cover for the entire Striking Force of twenty-one ships.

The Zero seen here, with the tail code A1-108, is pictured taking-off from *Akagi*, not for the attack on Midway but the earlier strike against Pearl Harbor during the morning of 7 December 1941. (USNHHC)

Below: A Nakajima B5N 'Kate' torpedo bomber is pictured taking off from the carrier *Akagi* during the filming of the Japanese propaganda film *From Pearl Harbor to Malaya*, circa March-April 1942. Its torpedo is a practice unit, as evidenced by its dented nose and lack of air box aerodynamic fins at the tail. (NARA)

05.45 hours   Japanese Aircraft Spotted
At 05.45 hours one of the patrolling Catalinas provided the news that everyone on Midway had been expecting. Sent in plain English was the following signal: 'Many planes heading Midway, bearing 320, distance 150.'[6] Five minutes later the Midway radar picked up the approaching aircraft at a distance of ninety-three miles and at an altitude of about 10,000 feet.

Slowly but surely a picture of the Japanese movements was beginning to emerge, though the key piece of information that still eluded the Americans was the location of the enemy carriers. That finally came at 05.52 hours, when, at last, the news reached Fletcher and Spruance that the Carrier Striking Force had been located by another of the Catalinas, such as the one shown above in 1942. (USNHHC)

05.55 hours   Enemy Aircraft Approach Midway
At 05.55 hours, the air-raid alarm was sounded at Midway, and by 06.00 hours, or shortly

after, every aircraft able to leave the ground, except one, was in the air – a total of 126 aircraft including the Catalinas that had taken off earlier.

The 1st, 4th and 5th Divisions of Marine Fighting Squadron 221 (VMF-221), with eight Brewster F2A-3 Buffalos and six Grumman F4F-3 Wildcat fighters, were vectored towards the approaching enemy aircraft, while the 2nd and 4th Divisions, totalling ten Buffalos, were ordered to orbit ten miles out in case another group of enemy aircraft should appear.

The weather was good and visibility excellent, and visual contact with the leading Japanese aircraft, such as the B5N1 'Kate', pictured on the bottom of the previous page was made less than fifteen minutes later. (USNHHC)

06.00 hours **The B-26s Takeoff**

The crews of the four B-26 Marauders at Midway, along with their commander Captain Collins, had been standing by their aircraft since 03.15 hours on the morning of 4 June. At 06.00 hours, with news of the approaching Japanese force, Collins was ordered to takeoff and attack the enemy carriers. Accompanied by six Grumman Avengers, the formation was on its way shortly afterwards. Below we see a B-26 with a Mark XIII aerial torpedo hung below its bomb bay on 11 May 1942. (NARA)

06.14 hours   'Tally Ho!'

Meanwhile, Captain John F. Carey, leading three aircraft of Marine Fighting Squadron 221 (VMF-221), which had deployed to Midway in December 1941, sighted some of the Japanese aircraft when they were about forty miles out from Midway. Carey spotted the large formation of Kate bombers at 12,000 feet, about 2,000 feet below him. The bombers were being screened by several divisions of Zero fighters flying above and just behind them.

Japanese carriers had no radar at this time, and the enemy formation was clearly unaware of the presence of the US aircraft in its vicinity. At 06.14 hours, Carey called out, 'Tally ho! Hawks at Angels twelve supported by fighters,' and swooped down on the attackers.

The above group photograph of VMF-221 personnel was taken after the battle. All but one of this group were survivors of the fighting on 4 June. Left to right, they have been identified as Captain Marion E. Carl, Captain Kirk Armistead, Major Raymond Scollin (of Marine Air Group 22), Captain Herbert T. Merrill, 2nd Lieutenant Charles M. Kunz, 2nd Lieutenant Charles Hughes, 2nd Lieutenant Hyde Phillips, Captain Philip R. White, and 2nd Lieutenant Roy A. Corry, Jr. (USNHHC)

Above: A Brewster F2A-3 Buffalo of VMF-221 being flown by 2nd Lieutenant Hank Ellis over North Island Naval Air Station, California, in November 1941. This actual aircraft was reportedly flown by 2nd Lieutenant Charles Hughes during the Battle of Midway - the Marine aviators flew a mix of twenty-one obsolescent F2A-3 and seven Grumman F4F-3 Wildcats on 4 June.

Though it survived due to Hughes' decision to return with a rough running engine, this aircraft was subsequently lost when it crashed into a swamp in Florida after the pilot baled out after an engine failure on 13 November 1942. (Courtesy of John F. Carey, USMC)

Below: Another representation by Norman Bel Geddes, this time depicting the lead elements of VMF-221's intercepting the Japanese air strike formation as it heads toward Midway on the morning of 4 June. One of VMF-221's pilots involved that day was 2nd Lieutenant William V. Brooks. He later gave this account of his part in the air battle:

'I was pilot of F2A-3, Bureau number 01523, Our division under Capt. Armistead was on standby duty at the end of the runway on the morning of June 4, 1942, from 0415 until 0615. At about 0600, the alarm sounded, and we took off. My division climbed rapidly, and I was having a hard time keeping up. I discovered afterwards that although my wheels indicator and hydraulic pressure indicator both registered "wheels up", they were in reality about 1/3 of the way down.

'We sighted the enemy at about 14,000 feet, I would say that there were 40 to 50 planes. At this time Lt. Sandoval was also dropping back. My radio was at this time putting out no volume, so I could not get the message from Zed. At 17,000 feet, Capt. Armistead led the attack followed closely by Capt. Humberd. They went down the left of the Vee, leaving two planes burning. Lt. Sandoval went down the right side of the formation and I followed. One of us got a plane from the right side of the Vee.

'At this time, I had completely lost sight of my division. As I started to pull up for another run on the bombers, I was attacked by two fighters. Because my wheels being jammed 1/3 way down, I could not out dive these planes, but managed to dodge them and fire a burst or so into them as they went past me and as I headed for the water. As I circled the island, the anti-aircraft fire drove them away. My tabs, instruments and cockpit were shot up to quite an extent at this time and I was intending to come in for a landing.'[7]

When he passed away in January 2010, Brooks was the last survivor of VMF-221 who had flown during the Battle of Midway. He was buried with full military honours in Bellview, Nebraska. (USNHHC)

Left: The commander of VMF-221 on 4 June, Major Floyd B. 'Red' Parks, USMC, pictured here, with the rank of Captain, at San Diego on 23 March 1942. 'Vastly outnumbered and outgunned,' notes the Missing Marines project, 'VMF-221 suffered heavy losses in the dogfight that followed. Major Parks was shot down by enemy fire; one account states that Parks managed to bail [sic] out but was strafed in his parachute. His remains could not be recovered.'[8] (USNHHC)

Below:
06.19 hours   Midway's Fighters Intercept the Japanese Bombers

Another of Norman Bel Geddes' representations, this image depicts the air battle between VMF-221's Buffalos and Wildcats and the Japanese Navy's carrier-borne Zero fighters, as the Marines attempted to intercept the Japanese bomber formation en route to attack Midway on the morning of 4 June. At 06.19 hours, a Midway outpost reported 'two planes falling in flames'. (USNHHC)

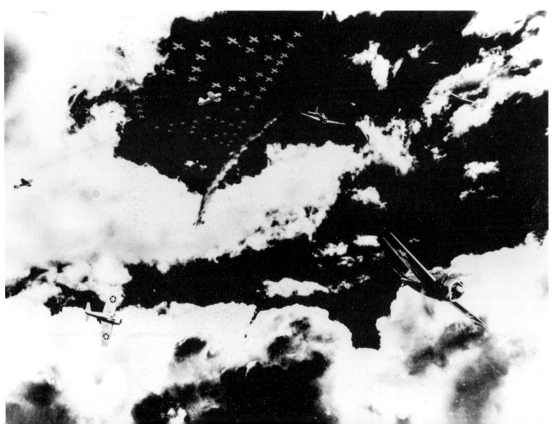

Above: Captain Marion Carl was among the pilots of VMF-221 who opened their 'tally' on 4 June when he shot down a Mitsubishi A6M Zero fighter. At the controls of a Grumman F4F-3 Wildcat, he also damaged two others.

Carl took off at 06.00 hours and climbed to an altitude of 14,000 feet, where he spotted a group of Japanese Zeros escorting Aichi D3A1 Type 99 bombers. Carl made an attack against one of the enemy fighters, which was flying 2,000 feet below him, and then immediately headed straight down at full throttle to avoid a pair of Zeros pursuing him. After evading them, he climbed to an altitude of 20,000 feet, and after observing no enemy aircraft, descended to 12,000 feet. The story is taken up by his post-action report:

'I saw three Zero fighters at a low altitude that were making a wide circle, so I came down in a 45° dive almost full throttle and had barely enough speed to drop in astern and to the inside of the circle made by one of the Zero fighters. I gave him a long burst, until he fell off on one wing and when last seen was out of control headed almost straight down with smoke streaming from the plane.

'The other two fighters had cut across and were closing on me, so I headed for a cloud. One fighter gave up the pursuit, but the other came on and started firing. He fired steadily for several seconds, but was shooting low, for I could see the tracers going by on both sides and slightly below me. Finally, I felt the impact of bullets striking the plane. He was gaining fast and had followed me through one cloud, so I cut the throttle, threw the plane into a skid, and he over ran me. I raked him with gun fire as he went by. He slid across in front and below me, and I shoved over sharply and pressed the trigger at the same time, but evidently the pushover was too sharp because none of my guns would fire. I dropped down astern the fighter and through a cloud. I saw no enemy plane thereafter.'[9]

Carl landed after being in the air for one-and-a-half hours. He estimated that he had used over 300 rounds in the combats. Carl was awarded the Navy Cross for his actions in that decisive battle. He is pictured here in the cockpit of an aeroplane at Anacostia Naval Air Station, Washington, D.C., circa 10 November 1942. (USNHHC)

Below: Personnel of VMF-221 pose for the camera in front of a camouflaged building at Ewa Mooring Mast Field, Oahu, on 14 July 1942. Most are survivors of the air action during the Battle of Midway.

Seated in the front row, left to right, are: Second Lieutenant William V. Brooks; Second Lieutenant John C. Musselman, Jr.; Captain Phillip R. White; Captain William C. Humberd; Captain Kirk Armistead; Captain Herbert T.

Merrill; Captain Marion E. Carl; and Second Lieutenant Clayton M. Canfield. Those standing in the back include, with one unidentified, Second Lieutenant Darrell D. Irwin, Second Lieutenant Hyde Phillips; Second Lieutenant Roy A. Corry, Jr. and Second Lieutenant Charles M. Kunz. Two of this group, Carl and Kunz, would become Aces by the end of the war.

Those VMF-221 pilots who survived the events of 4 June 1942, claimed eleven enemy aircraft shot down, with one probably shot down, and four others damaged. Japanese records confirm that eleven aircraft were shot down by Marine aircraft and anti-aircraft gunners, with fourteen others badly damaged. Fourteen of the VMF-221's pilots, including its CO, were killed in action. Five VMF-221 enlisted men died on the ground in the bombing of Midway by enemy aircraft.[10] (USNHHC)

Below: A damaged and partially disassembled Grumman F4F-3 Wildcat pictured on Sand Island, Midway, after the attack on 4 June. This Wildcat was flown by Captain John F. Carey, USMC, one of the VMF-221 pilots, during the squadron's attack on incoming Japanese raiders on the morning of 4 June. Carey was wounded in this action.

Several other planes are visible in the right background, including F2A-3 Buffalos. This view was taken looking roughly south-west from near the foot of the Sand Island pier. The seaplane hangar, which was heavily damaged by Japanese bombs that day, is in the left background. (USNHHC)

Opposite page top: Norman Bel Geddes' depiction of the Japanese carrier aircraft attack on Midway in the morning of 4 June 1942. Two of the attackers are shown at the left, a third bottom right. Eastern Island airfield is under attack in the lower centre. Sand Island is in the upper left centre, with hits visible in the vicinity of the seaplane hangar. (USNHHC)

Below: A painting by Griffith Baily Coale that depicts US Navy PT (short for Patrol Torpedo) boats during Japanese aircraft attacks on Midway. The original caption states that 'the PT's are skimming about, darting here, dodging there, manoeuvring between the rows of machine-gun splashes, incessantly firing their twin pairs [of] 50 caliber guns'. (USNHHC)

06.56 hours End of the Japanese Attack upon Midway

Burning oil tanks on Sand Island, Midway, following the Japanese air attack delivered on the morning of 4 June 1942. These tanks were located near what was then the southern shore of Sand Island. This view looks inland from the vicinity of the beach. The end of the attack was announced at 06.56 hours. (USNHHC)

Another scene of destruction on Sand Island, Midway, following the Japanese attack. This view, probably photographed from the powerplant roof, looks roughly south-west, along what was then Sand Island's southern shore. The building in the foreground is the laundry, which was badly damaged by a bomb. Oil tanks are burning in the distance. (NARA)

29

Above: Firefighting crews at work in the badly damaged seaplane hangar on Sand Island. (NARA)

Chapter 3

ATTACKING THE JAPANESE FLEET

4 June 1942

07.00 hours   The US Carriers Prepare to Fight Back

In accordance with Japanese carrier doctrine at the time, Admiral Nagumo had kept half of his aircraft in reserve. Whilst the Midway attackers were returning, Nagumo considered his next move, which included the possibility of a second strike on the atoll. The Americans, however, were taking matters into their own hands.

Rear Admiral Fletcher, benefiting from the PBY sighting reports obtained earlier that morning, ordered his carriers to launch their aircraft against the Japanese as soon as was practical. This process began at 07.00 hours, with USS *Enterprise* and USS *Hornet* having completed the task by 07.55 hours; USS *Yorktown*, initially held in reserve in case any other Japanese carriers were spotted, followed by 09.08 hours. The aircraft that would deliver the crushing blow at Midway were on their way.

This picture depicts the preparations underway on the flight deck of USS *Enterprise* just prior to 07.00 hours. The aircraft, Douglas TBD-1 Devastators, are from the US Navy's Torpedo Squadron 6 (VT-6). Eleven of the fourteen TBDs launched from *Enterprise* are visible in this photograph. Three more TBDs and ten Grumman F4F-4 Wildcat fighters still need to be pushed into position before launching can begin.

The TBD in the left front is Number Two, flown by Ensign Severin L. Rombach and Aviation Radioman 2nd Class W.F. Glenn. Along with eight other VT-6 aircraft, this plane and its crew were lost attacking the Japanese aircraft carriers little more than two hours after the picture was taken.

The heavy cruiser USS *Pensacola* is in the right distance. A destroyer on the anti-aircraft picket can be seen at left. (NARA)

07.06 hours   *Enterprise* **Launches its Aircraft**
Launching from the USS *Enterprise* began just six minutes after the order had been given. The order of launching was: 1) fighters to provide protection of the carrier; 2) dive bombers; 3) torpedo bombers; and 4) fighters to protect the torpedo bombers. Their target was the Japanese Carrier Striking Force. The great trap was about to be sprung.

This view of the USS *Enterprise* was taken from the cockpit of an SBD (Scout Bomber Douglas) Dauntless just after it had left the flight deck. Though this photograph was taken after Midway, it gives some indication of what it was like to take off from a carrier at sea. (USNHHC)

At the same time as *Enterprise*, *Hornet* also began launching its Air Group of thirty-five Dauntless bombers, each armed with 500-pound bombs, fifteen torpedo bombers and ten fighters. This photograph, taken at Ford Island Naval Air Station, shows USS *Hornet* arriving at Pearl Harbor on 26 May 1942. She left just two days later to take part in the Battle of Midway. Note the two aircraft towing tractors parked in the foreground. (US Navy)

USS *Yorktown*'s Air Group was initially held back in reserve as only two enemy carriers had been spotted thus far and the other two were likely to be somewhere within striking range. This photograph of the 25,900-ton, 770-feet long *Yorktown*, which was capable of more than thirty-two knots, shows its Air Group lined up on the flight deck in December 1940. (USNHHC)

Above:

07.05 hours   Midway-based   Bombers Attack the Japanese Fleet

Captain James Collins and his aircrews from the 18th Reconnaissance Squadron, 22nd Bombardment Group USAAF had been sleeping beside their four B-26 Marauders at Midway when the alert sounded at 05.30 hours to signal the enemy's approach. The bombers' engines were being warmed up on the Eastern Island runway when the Army liaison officer arrived to hand Captain Collins the order to attack the Japanese carriers and provide him with details of bearing, distance, and speed of the carriers.

The four B-26s from Midway and six Avengers of the US Navy's Torpedo Squadron 8 (VT-8) made contact with the Japanese carrier force at 07.05 hours. The Japanese immediately launched all of their Zero fighters. As the American bombers approached the Striking Force, the picket destroyers opened fire, followed moments later by the guns of the battleship *Kirishima* (ordered in 1911, originally as a battlecruiser, she was designed by the British naval engineer George Thurston).

This unusual view of a Marauder, taken after the Battle of Midway, shows an aircraft operating in the European theatre. (USAF)

Below: Grumman F4F-4 Wildcats of *Yorktown*'s Fighting Squadron Three (VF-3) receiving maintenance in a revetment at Naval Air Station, Kaneohe, Oahu, on 29 May 1942, shortly before the unit joined USS *Yorktown*. (NARA)

Above: As the B-26s began their run towards the Japanese ships, they were engaged head-on by six Zero fighters, and two of the bombers were shot down. One of these managed to release its torpedo towards one of the carriers before crashing onto the flight deck and being hurled into the sea. Because of the swarm of some fifty Zeros defending the carrier group, Captain James Collins did not loiter to observe the results of his attack, but it was thought that two of the torpedoes struck the bow area of the carrier *Hiryu*.

One of the two B-26s that returned from the attack crashed on landing. At the same time, both were so badly shot up that they could no longer take part in the battle.

Seen here is the crew of 1st Lieutenant James 'Jim' Muri's B-26, which made a torpedo attack on a Japanese aircraft carrier during the early morning of 4 June 1942. The plane was found to have more than 500 bullet holes when it landed back at Midway. 1st Lieutenant Muri is in the front row, second from left.

Muri's crew dropped a torpedo at a range of about 450 yards from one of the carriers at a height of 150 feet, before pulling up over the ship. In fact, there was no damage reported by any of the carriers in the attack by the B-26s. (USNHHC)

Below: The honour of being the first US Navy aircraft to engage the Japanese fleet on 4 June 1942, fell to six Avengers of VT-8. It was just prior to Midway that VT-8 began to re-equip with the Grumman TBF-1 Avenger. When USS *Hornet* had sailed for the Pacific, a detachment from VT-8 remained at Norfolk, Virginia, to receive the first of the new aircraft.

Commanded by Lieutenant Harold 'Swede' Larson, this detachment arrived at Pearl Harbor the day after *Hornet* had departed for Midway; the rest of the squadron on the carrier was still

equipped with the older, slower Douglas TBD Devastator. As a result, led by Lieutenant Langdon K. Fieberling, six of VT-8's Avengers were flown direct to Midway. These six Avengers flew from Midway on the morning of 4 June with the B-26 bombers and attacked the

Japanese ships shortly after the B-26s.

This broadside view of *Hornet* was taken at Naval Operating Base Norfolk, Virginia, in February 1942. Amongst the aircraft ranged on the carrier's flight deck are Douglas TBD-1s of VT-8. (USNHHC)

Above: One of the six Avengers delivered to Lieutenant Harold 'Swede' Larson's detachment from VT-8. This aircraft, coded 8-T-1 and with the Bureau No.00380, was one of the six that went into action at Midway, being flown by Ensign Albert Kyle 'Bert' Earnest. (US Navy)

Below: Personnel of VT-8 photographed on board USS *Hornet* in mid-May 1942, shortly before the Battle of Midway. In the front row, left to right, are Ensign Harold J. Ellison, Ensign Henry R. Kenyon, Ensign John P. Gray, Ensign George H. Gay, Jr. (circled), Lieutenant (Junior Grade) Jeff D. Woodson, Ensign William W. Creamer, and Aviation Pilot First Class Robert B. Miles. The men in the back row, again left to right, are Lieutenant James C. Owens, Jr., Ensign E.L. Fayle, Lieutenant Commander John C. Waldron (the squadron's Commanding Officer), Lieutenant Raymond A. Moore, Ensign Ulvert M. Moore, Ensign William R. Evans, Ensign Grant W. Teats, and Lieutenant (Junior Grade) George M. Campbell. (USNHHC)

07.10 hours   **US Navy Torpedo Bombers Attack**

Following the B-26s in, the Avengers of VT-8 attacked without fighter cover. In the battle that followed, five of the aircraft were shot down.

The pilot of the sixth, Ensign Albert Earnest, managed to nurse his badly damaged Avenger, 8-T-1, back to Midway – when the picture above was taken. Of the two men in Earnest's crew, Radioman 3rd Class Harrier H. Ferrier survived, whilst Seaman 1st Class Jay D. Manning, who was operating the .50 calibre machine-gun turret, was killed during the combats with Japanese fighters during the attack. (USNHHC)

Below: Ensign Albert Earnest's Avenger, 8-T-1, photographed having been lifted back up on its undercarriage at Midway.

All six VT-8 Avenger pilots earned the Navy Cross for their part in the Battle of Midway, as well as two enlisted members of their crews. (USNHHC)

Below: A close-up of the badly shot-up turret of Ensign Albert Earnest's Avenger, coded 8-T-1. It was in this turret that Seaman 1st Class Jay Darrell Manning was killed during the combat with Japanese fighters during the attack, as Harrier Ferrier later recalled: 'On the second firing pass by the attacking Zeros, our turret gunner, Manning, was hit and his turret put out of action. The sight of his slumped and lifeless body startled me. Quite suddenly, I was a scared, mature old man at 17. I had never seen death before, and here in one awesome moment my friends and I were face-to-face with it.'[11]

Manning's body was recovered from this turret and he was formally buried at sea off Midway Island on 5 June, along with others who were killed by Japanese aircraft during the bombing attack the previous day.

For his actions, Manning was posthumously awarded the Distinguished Flying Cross, 'for extraordinary achievement while participating

in aerial flight as free machine gunner of a Torpedo Plane in action against enemy Japanese forces in the Battle of Midway, 4 and 5 June 1942. In the initial attack upon an enemy aircraft carrier, Aviation Machinist's Mate Third Class Manning, with utter disregard for his own personal safety, effectively manned his machine gun in the face of a tremendous barrage of fire from numerous Japanese fighter planes and anti-aircraft batteries.

His courageous determination and devotion to duty were in keeping with the highest traditions of the United States Naval Service. He gallantly gave his life for his country.'[12] (USNHHC)

Below: Ensign Albert Earnest's Avenger photographed near the foot of the Sand Island pier, Midway, on 24 June 1942, prior to shipment to the United States for evaluation. (USNHHC)

USS *Enterprise* steaming at high speed at about 07.25 hours on 4 June, as seen from the cruiser USS *Pensacola* after the last of the carrier's Air Group had flown off to engage the enemy. (USNHHC)

Below: Another unit based at Midway that was involved in the aerial attacks on 4 June was Marine Scout Bombing Squadron 241, or VMSB-241. This squadron had arrived at Midway in December 1941, and in doing so had set a new record. One of only two USMC squadrons that were equipped with the Marine-specific SB2U-3 variant of the Vought Vindicator, VMSB-241 had flown from Hawaii to Midway, undertaking the longest overwater flight by a single-engine aircraft on record at that time. With the aircraft fitted with an extra fuel tank and supported by a Catalina, the squadron arrived at Midway without the loss of a single aircraft.

This picture of the personnel of VMSB-241 was taken on Midway between 17 April and 28 May 1942. In the front row, left to right, are: 2nd Lieutenant Albert W. Tweedy; 1st Lieutenant Bruce Posser (wearing sandals); Major Lofton R. Henderson, USMC (the Commanding Officer); Captain Leo R. Smith, USMC; and 1st Lieutenant Elmer G. Gidden, Jr. In the middle row, are: 2nd Lieutenant Thomay J. Gratzek; 2nd Lieutenant Robert W. Vaupell; 1st Lieutenant Daniel Iverson, Jr.; 2nd Lieutenant Jese D. Rollow, Jr.; 2nd Lieutenant Harold G. Schlendering; and Technical Sergeant (NAP) Clyde H. Stamps, USMC. The men in the rear row are: 2nd Lieutenant Maurice A. Ward; 1st Lieutenant Richard L Blain; 2nd Lieutenant Sumner H. Whitten; 2nd Lieutenant Thomas F. Moore, Jr.; 1st Lieutenant Armond M. DeLalio; 2nd Lieutenant Bruce Ek; 1st Lieutenant Leon M. Williamson; 1st Lieutenant Richard E. Fleming; 2nd Lieutenant Robert J. Bear; MARGUN (NAP) Howard C. Fraser, USMC; and 2nd Lieutenant Bruno P. Hagedorn. Those men marked with an 'X' were killed during the Battle of Midway, 4-6 June 1942. (US Navy)

07.55 hours　　　　　　　　**VMSB-241's**
First Wave Attacks

Whilst at Midway, VMSB-241 divided into two groups. The first was equipped with sixteen Douglas SBD Dauntlesses commanded by Major Lofton R. Henderson, the squadron CO; the second, of eleven Vindicators was led by Major Benjamin W. Norris.

'At 0755, through broken cloud formations below them,' wrote Lieutenant Colonel R.D. Heinl, Jr., an official US historian, 'the Marine pilots sighted their target, Admiral Nagumo's striking force, four carriers, battleships, and numerous smaller combatant ships. Just below was the 26,900-ton *Akagi*, and it was this ship which Major Henderson determined to attack.

'Because of the relative unfamiliarity of most of his pilots with the SBD-2 (a result of the curtailed fuel allowances during the week before), Henderson planned on a glide- rather than a dive-bombing run, and commenced a let-down to 4,000 feet, from which he intended to launch his attack. As the SBDs spiralled down, they began receiving violent fighter attacks from Nakajima 97s and Zeros, which were momentarily reinforced by more fighters from the carriers below. Aboard the *Akagi*, their target, Marine pilots could see three fighters take off. Heavy anti-aircraft fire began to thicken the air, and, below, the *Akagi* commenced evasive maneuvers at flank speed.'[13]

One of the Marine pilots was Captain Elmer G. Glidden, leader of the second division in Major Henderson's group: 'The first (enemy fighter) attacks were directed at the squadron leader in an attempt to put him out of action. After about two passes, one of the enemy put several shots through the plane of Major Henderson, and his plane started to burn. From the actions of the leader it was apparent that he was hit and out of action. I was leader of the second box immediately behind the Major. As soon as it was apparent that the Major was out of action, I took over the lead and continued the attack. Fighter attacks were heavy, so I led the squadron down through a protecting layer of clouds and gave the signal to attack. On emerging from the cloud-bank the enemy carrier was directly below the squadron, and all planes made their runs. The diving interval was about 5 seconds.

'Immediately after coming out from the protection of the clouds, the squadron was attacked again by fighter planes and heavy AA. After making my run, I kept heading on for the water, and I headed on an approximate bearing home. Looking back, I saw two hits and one miss that was right alongside the bow. The carrier was starting to smoke.'[14]

Lieutenant Colonel R.D. Heinl notes that 'Captain Glidden's observation of the two

bomb hits (each by a 500-pound bomb) is confirmed by the commanding officer of the *Akagi*, who was interrogated after the war, as well as by other enemy sources. Until the end of hostilities, there had been some question as to which of the enemy carriers VMSB-241 had actually hit, but the *Akagi*'s records, together with Admiral Nagumo's report of the battle, jibe quite accurately with the reports of the Marine squadron.

'According to the Nagumo report, at 0800 the *Akagi* sighted "16 enemy planes bearing 85°, elevation 7°, distant 17,000 meters." At 0805, further, she launched three fighters, which were evidently those noticed taking off by the Marine pilots. Prior to 0810, reports of other ships in the task force indicated that *Akagi* had received bomb hits. Under interrogation, her Captain stated that his ship's first damage had occurred by fire as a result of "two bombs by dive bombing, about 2 hours after sunrise (one started fire at after elevator). Planes were loaded up with bombs inside the hangar and caught fire." Since sunrise that day took place prior to 0600, it could only have been the 16 Marine dive-bombers which drew first blood from the enemy carriers.'

The poor-quality photograph above shows a Vought SB2U-3 Vindicator dive bomber of VMSB-241 taking off from Eastern Island, Midway. It is being flown by 2nd Lieutenant George T. Lumpkin (pilot) and Private First Class. George A. Toms (gunner).

Above: The crews of VMSB-241's first group withdrew at masthead level or lower in an effort to escape the incessant Japanese fighter attacks. The enemy pilots pursued the torpedo bombers for some distance, and so devastating were the combats that only eight of the original group landed back at Midway. For their part, the rear gunners of this strike group are credited with having shot down four enemy fighters plus two additional probables.

All of the VMSB-241 aircraft that returned had sustained battle damage of varying degrees, mostly extensive. This SBD-2, Bureau Number 2106, is one of those aircraft. Having arrived at Midway on 26 May 1942, being delivered by the aircraft transport USS *Kitty Hawk*, it was flown by 1st Lieutenant David Iverson (pilot) and PF1c Wallace Reid (rear gunner) on 4 June 1942. After unsuccessfully attacking the carrier *Hiryu*, Iverson returned to Midway (when this picture was taken) where it was found that enemy fire had holed the aircraft more than 200 times. (US National Museum of Naval Aviation)

Left: Another view of 1st Lieutenant David Iverson's SBD-2 after its return to Midway. Some of the damage caused by the Japanese aircraft and ships can be clearly seen. Returned to the US, 2106 was eventually repaired and returned to service. It ditched in Lake Michigan whilst trying to land on a training carrier on 11 June 1943. Recovered in 1994, following extensive restoration it went on display at the US National Museum of Naval Aviation at Pensacola, Florida, where it can be seen to this day. (US National Museum of Naval Aviation)

08.10 hours   *Soryu* **Attacked**

The B-17s of Flight 92 were the next to strike the Japanese carriers. This group of fifteen planes was commanded by Lieutenant Colonel Sweeney. Two bombers carried eight 600lb bombs each, the rest eight 500lb bombs. These aircraft had cleared Midway about 04.15 hours, shortly after the patrol planes had been sent out. They were proceeding to the west to attack the enemy forces sighted the preceding day, when a message was received in plain language reporting the discovery of the enemy carrier force on bearing 325 degrees from Midway.

Climbing to 20,000 feet, the B-17s changed course to find the carriers. The enemy force was located at 07.32 hours, but the carriers, circling under a cloud formation, were not found until 08.10 hours. The bombers had skirted the fleet and approached from the northwest, i.e., from the stern of the targets. They attacked by flights, two elements concentrating on each of two carriers and a single element on a third. Anti-aircraft fire was heavy and found the altitude, but was generally behind the attackers. The Japanese fighters did not press home their attacks, which were ineffectual.

The results of this attack were reported to be three hits on two carriers. It is probable that two of these hits were on *Soryu*. In the image below we can see *Soryu* circling while under high-level bombing attack by the B-17s shortly after 08.00 hours. (USAF)

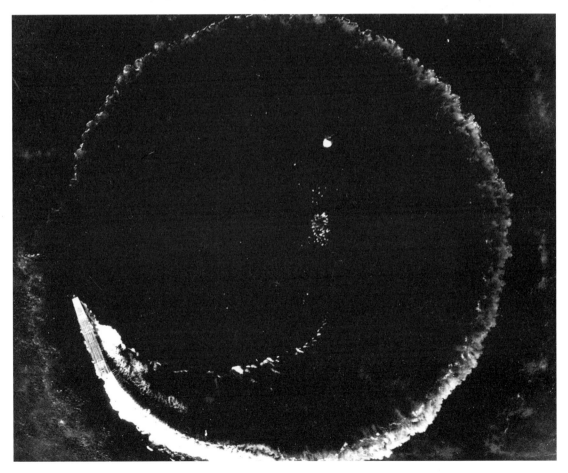

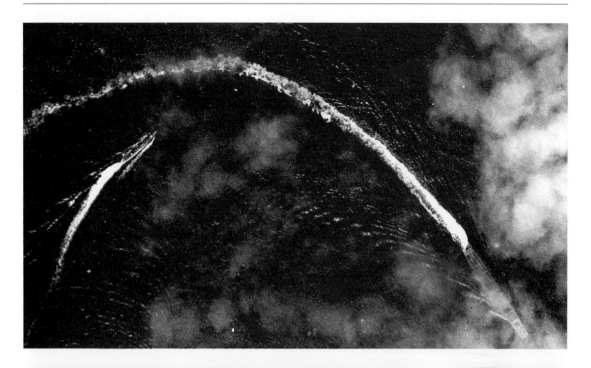

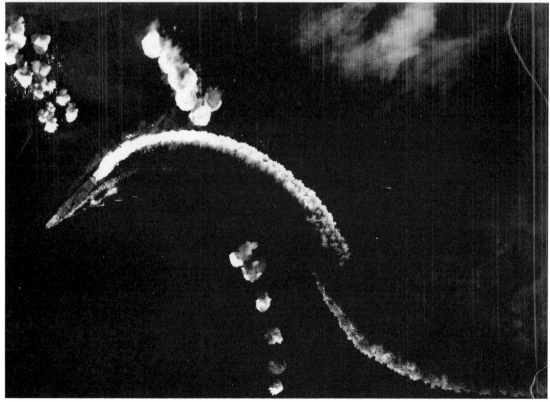

Opposite page top: A similar scene to that depicted in the previous image, though on this occasion it is the carrier Akagi and an escorting destroyer that are taking evasive action while under a high-level bombing attack by the B-17s shortly after 08.00 hours, 4 June 1942. (USAF)

Opposite page bottom: The Japanese carrier *Hiryu* is seen here manoeuvring to avoid three sticks of bombs dropped during a high-level attack by the B-17s at about 08.12 hours. (USAF)

08.20 hours   VMSB-241's Second Attack
Scarcely had the B-17s left when the second part of VMSB-241 forces from Midway, consisting of eleven Vought SB2U Vindicators under the command of Major Morris, arrived on the scene. Almost immediately, Japanese fighters were encountered at 13,000 feet. In fact, the opposition from these was so severe that the Vindicators struggled to bomb any of the carriers. Major Norris, for example, decided not to press the search for the carriers, but chose a battleship as his target.

Captain Armond H. Delalio was one of the Vindicator pilots: 'We emerged from clouds at 2,000 feet and there lay a large aircraft carrier slightly off to my left. We peeled off and dove in very close intervals; the carrier was taking violent avoiding action and AA fire seemed very heavy. I released my bomb at low altitude and scooted on the water, weaving as I went. I looked to see if the carrier was damaged and observed the forward part of the deck to be smoking heavily.

'At this point I was made aware of a fighter on my tail. He was very close in and bullets were ripping through and past my plane. My gunner, Corporal John H. Moore, USMC, was doing a good job on the free gun and after five minutes of fire, the fighter ceased firing. Corporal Moore stated that he got the fighter and that he was wounded in the leg.'[15] Three near misses were reported by *Kaga* off its stern and the battleship *Haruna* was straddled by six bombs, but no Japanese ships were hit.

The USMC Vought SB2U Vindicator seen here was pictured in flight in July 1941. (USNHHC)

08.30 hours 'Launch Attack Force Immediately'

While Nagumo's fighters were successfully fending off the American bombers, the Japanese admiral had to consider his next move, still blissfully unaware of the presence of the US carriers. Of the 108 Japanese aircraft involved in the first attack upon Midway, eleven had been destroyed, fourteen had been heavily damaged, and twenty-nine less severely damaged. The returning pilots stated that they had failed to put Henderson Field out of use and that a second strike would be necessary to neutralise Midway's defences before the Occupation Force attempted its landing, scheduled for 7 June. Consequently, as the B-26 torpedo attack was ending, Nagumo ordered the planes of the second wave, which had been armed with torpedoes for an attack on naval vessels as a precaution, to re-arm with bombs for a second attack on Midway. As the only American aerial attacks had come from land-based aircraft, the Japanese admiral was satisfied that, as predicted, there was no enemy surface force for him to worry about.

The order to re-arm had barely been given before a report came in from a pilot of a reconnaissance aircraft operating from the Japanese heavy cruiser *Tone* that he had sighted what appeared to be an enemy force of ten surface ships about 240 miles from Midway. The pilot was asked to state what type of ships the force was composed of. It was thirty minutes before a reply was received: 'Enemy is composed of five cruisers and five destroyers', followed at 08.20 hours with the astonishing information that, 'The enemy is accompanied by what appears to be a carrier'. This carrier was the USS *Yorktown*. This information changed everything. Here was a chance to sink an American carrier.

Admiral Nagumo contemplated whether or not he should clear his carriers' decks to allow the aircraft returning from the attack on Midway to land, doing so by launching his dive and torpedo bombers at the American warships without fighter cover (the Zeros were fully occupied dealing with the attacks by the Midway aircraft), or allow the returning aircraft to re-arm and refuel before reorganising his force to launch a fully-coordinated 'grand' attack. On his flagship *Hiryu*, Rear Admiral Yamaguchi was in no doubt. He relayed a signal via the destroyer *Nowaki* to his commander: 'Consider it advisable to launch attack force immediately.'[16]

The picture on the previous pages show the USS *Yorktown* in Dry Dock No.1 at the Pearl Harbor Naval Shipyard on 29 May 1942. At the time this photograph was taken she was receiving urgent repairs for damage received in the Battle of Coral Sea, but sailed the following day to participate in the Battle of Midway.

**08.40 hours   USS *Yorktown* Launches
                       its Air Group**

On the USS *Yorktown*, meanwhile, there was a very real concern that the carrier might be caught by the Japanese with her planes on deck, although no more enemy carriers had been reported. Therefore, at about 08.40 hours all twelve Douglas TBD-1 Devastators of

Torpedo Squadron Three (VT-3) were launched, along with half of the bomber squadron, VB-3, and six fighters. The seventeen remaining scout bombers were held in reserve in the hope that the other two enemy carriers might be found. Each torpedo plane carried one Mk.XIII torpedo and each bomber one 1,000lb bomb.

The torpedo planes immediately headed for the target. The scout bombers were ordered to circle for twelve minutes before proceeding to overtake the torpedo planes. To conserve fuel, the fighters were not launched till 09.05 hours. The three squadrons effected rendezvous at 09.45 hours. It is one of *Yorktown*'s Devastators that is shown here en route to attack the Japanese carrier force during the morning of 4 June 1942. (NARA)

Opposite page: A Grumman F4F-4 Wildcat fighter (Bureau No.5244) takes off from *Yorktown* to form part of the fighter cover for the torpedo and bomber squadrons. This aircraft, Number 13 of VF-3, was flown by the squadron's Executive Officer, Lieutenant (Junior Grade) William N. Leonard. Photographed by Photographer Second Class William G. Roy, from the carrier's forecastle. (USNHHC)

09.20 hours — The Devastators of VT-8 Attack

Led by Lieutenant Commander John C. Waldron, the Douglas TBD Devastators of VT-8 had flown at a lower altitude and became separated from the rest of the group, although there were only scattered clouds. This squadron, no longer with any fighter protection, turned north and, at about 09.20 hours found the carriers *Akagi*, *Kaga*, *Hiryu* and *Soryu*. Without hesitation they swooped down towards the Japanese Striking Force.

As the Devastators of VT-8 dived towards the enemy ships they encountered overwhelming fighter opposition. A moment later they ran into a heavy screen of anti-aircraft fire thrown up by the destroyers and cruisers. With no fighters to protect them from the Zeros, one by one the Devastators were shot out of the sky. Of the fifteen planes that had taken off from *Hornet*, none returned.

One pilot, Ensign George H. Gay, survived after he crashed near *Akagi*, though his rear gunner, ARM3c George Arthur Field, had been killed. By hiding under a floating seat cushion and refraining from inflating his life raft until after dark, he saved his own life and witnessed the succeeding attacks by the US carrier forces. Gay, pictured above right, gave the following account of the attack:

'When I first saw the Japanese carriers, one of them was afire and another ship had a fire aboard and I thought that there was a battle in progress, and we were late. I was a little bit impatient that we didn't get right on in there then, and when it finally turned out that we got close enough in that we could make a contact report and describe what we could see, the Zeros jumped on us and it was too late.

'They turned out against us in full strength and I figured that there was about 35 of them, I understand, that is I found out later, that they operated Fighter Squadrons in numbers of about 32 and I guess it was one of those 32-plane squadrons that got us. It's been a very

general opinion that the anti-aircraft fire shot our boys down and that's not true. I don't think that any of our planes were damaged, even touched by anti-aircraft fire; the fighters, the Zeros, shot down everyone of them, and by the time we got in to where the anti-aircraft fire began to get hot, the fighters all left us … I was the only one close enough to get any real hot anti-aircraft fire, and I don't think it even touched me and I went right through it, right over the ship.'[17] (USNHHC)

Opposite page: After some thirty hours in the water, Ensign Gay was rescued by the crew of a US Navy Catalina. Gay was the only survivor of the VT-8s Devastator crews that attacked the Japanese at Midway. He is pictured here whilst recovering at the naval hospital at Pearl Harbor reading a copy of the *Honolulu Star-Bulletin* newspaper featuring accounts of the battle. In his memoir, *Sole Survivor*, Gay indicates that this photograph was probably taken on 7 June 1942, following an operation to repair his injured left hand and a meeting with Admiral Chester W. Nimitz. (US National Museum of the US Navy)

Above: An earlier photograph of Douglas Devastator, Bureau Number 0284, of VT-5 after a landing accident on USS *Yorktown*. Ultimately assigned to VT-8, this was one of the aircraft lost in the attack upon the Japanese carriers. (USNHHC)

Right: Another of VT-8's Devastators which were lost in the attack on the carriers. With the Bureau Number 0297, it is shown here following an earlier accident while landing on *Yorktown*. (USNHHC)

10.00 hours   **VT-6 Spot the**
                        Japanese Carriers

Ensign Gay had been in the water long before the *Enterprise* and *Yorktown* groups arrived to continue the assault upon the Japanese Striking Force. The torpedo squadron from USS *Enterprise*, VT-6, had been launched at about 07.49 hours and proceeded independently to the target. On the way it lost its fighter escort of ten F4F-4s, which later joined the *Yorktown*'s torpedo squadron, so that VT-6 also launched its attack without protection. At about 10.00

hours it sighted the Japanese fleet. As they circled round to make their attack run, the Douglas TBD-1 Devastators were exposed to heavy anti-aircraft and fighter fire. Nevertheless, they pressed on through possibly as many as twenty-five Japanese fighters, but few of them were able to deliver their torpedoes, and none scored a direct hit.

This view of part of USS *Enterprise*'s flight deck, taken on 11 April 1942, includes a number of VT-6's Devastators, as well as F4Fs of VF-6. (USNHHC)

USS *Enterprise*'s Douglas TBD-1 Devastator-equipped VT-6 pictured flying in formation before the start of the war. The aircraft closest to the camera, that with the Bureau Number 1511, was lost while assigned to VT-3 during the Battle of Midway. (USNHHC)

10.10 hours   ***Yorktown's* Torpedo Bombers Strike**

At almost the same time that *Enterprise*'s VT-6 attacked the Japanese carriers, VT-3 delivered its attack, but to no effect, with ten out of its twelve Devastators being shot down. The image of the squadron's pilots seen above was taken at the Naval Air Station Kaneohe, Hawaii, in late May 1942, just before the Battle of Midway. Most of these men did survive the battle. (USNHHC)

Right: The commanding officer of VT-3, Lieutenant Commander Lance E. Massey, in the cockpit of his Devastator at Naval Air Station Ford Island, Pearl Harbor, on 24 May 1942. Note the Victory flag marking representing the sinking of a Japanese ship during the Marshall Islands Raid on 1 February 1942, when he was Executive Officer of VT-6 on USS *Enterprise*. For his heroism in pursuing the attack on *Soryu* at Midway, Massey was posthumously awarded the Navy Cross. (USNHHC)

Right: Another of VT-3's pilots to die at Midway was Ensign Wesley Osmus – pictured here just prior to his enlistment in March 1940. Osmus's Devastator was the last in the squadron's formation on 4 June – but was the first to be hit. When the aircraft's fuel tank was hit and burst into flames, Osmus, the pilot, was able to bale out.

His radioman-gunner, Benjamin R. Dodson, Jnr., did not follow. Either dead or badly wounded, Dodson went down with the blazing aircraft.

Osmus was rescued from the sea by the Japanese destroyer *Arashi*. However, after interrogating him, Ensign Osmus was attacked and his body dumped in the sea.

The fate of the US aviator only came to light after the war when the US Navy gained access to the Battle of Midway post-action report compiled by Admiral Nagumo. The circumstances of the young pilot's death while on board Arashi were then investigated as a possible war crime.

It was found that it was *Arashi*'s captain, Watanabe Yasumasa, who gave the order for Osmus to be executed. Osmus was, therefore, taken to the stern of the destroyer and thrown overboard, but he managed to grab the chain railing. A fire axe was then fetched and employed to complete the murder of the young pilot whose body fell into the sea.[18] (USNHHC)

Right: Seven of the twelve Devastator torpedo bombers of VT-3 were shot down before they could release their torpedoes. Amongst those was that of Lieutenant Patrick H. Hart USN, who posthumously received the Navy Cross for heroism in persisting with his attack in the face of heavy opposition from the Japanese fighters.

His mother, Mrs Emma Hart, sponsored the building of a Fletcher-class destroyer which was named *Hart* (DD-594) in honour of her son. (USNHHC)

12.22 hours   *Enterprise* **Air Group Attack**
The attacks by the US torpedo bombers confirmed the reports of a carrier in the area. At this stage of the battle Nagumo's four carriers were undamaged and there was every prospect that he could strike a major blow against the Americans if he was able to swiftly counter-attack. There was no time to lose, and, one after another, planes were hoisted from *Akagi*'s hangar and quickly arranged on the flight deck. Soon, all the aircraft were warming up their engines on the packed flight deck.

At 10.20 hours the admiral gave the order to launch. But then out of the clouds came

Enterprise's and *Yorktown*'s bomber groups. They promptly began a series of attacks that over the course of the next few minutes were to change the course of the war in the Pacific.

While the American torpedo bombers had failed to hit any of Nagumo's carriers, they had dislocated the Japanese fighters providing the vital cover and many of the Zeros were low on ammunition and fuel. The carriers were horribly exposed and about to be wrecked.

Lieutenant Wade McClusky was *Enterprise*'s Air Group commander and he led Scouting Six, VS-6, and Bombing Six, VB-6, in the attack against *Kaga* and *Akagi*. McClusky had been told to maintain radio silence until the enemy ships had been sighted and to deliver a group attack. The Air Group was supposed to have fighter protection, but poor coordination led to the bombers flying unsupported. McClusky reached the area where the Japanese fleet was supposed to be at 11.20 hours, but the sea was empty.

McClusky assessed his fuel reserves and considered that he could fly on for possibly another hour, but no more, and then he would have to turn back. He calculated that as the enemy ships could not be between him and Midway, he decided to fly west for thirty-five miles, then to turn north-west in the precise reverse of the original Japanese course. That decision of McClusky's, in the words of Admiral Nimitz, 'decided the fate of our carrier task force and our forces at Midway'.

At 11.55 hours, just as McClusky was about to turn north-west, he spotted the Japanese destroyer *Arashi* travelling at full speed. Thinking that it might lead him to the Striking Force, McClusky followed. Ten minutes later his hunch paid off.

'Peering through my binoculars, which were practically glued to my eyes, I saw dead ahead about 35 miles distant the welcome sight of the Jap carrier striking force,' recalled McClusky. 'They were in what appeared to be a circular disposition with four carriers in the center, well-spaced, and an outer screen of six to eight destroyers and inner support ships composed of two battleships and either four or six cruisers.

'I then broke radio silence and reported the contact to the *Enterprise*. Immediately thereafter I gave attack instructions to my group. Figuring that possibly the *Hornet* group commander would make the same decision that I had, it seemed best to concentrate my two squadrons on two carriers. Any greater division of the bomb-load we had might spread out the damage, but I believed would not sink or completely put out of action more than two. Picking the two nearest carriers in the line of approach, I ordered Scouting Six to follow my section in attacking the carrier on the immediate left and Bombing Six to take the right-hand carrier.'

McClusky was amazed to find the carriers with no fighters in the air and that he had a free run at the Japanese ships. 'It was 1222 when I started the attack, rolling in a half-roll and coming to a steep 70 degree dive. About halfway down, anti-aircraft fire began booming around us - our approach being a complete surprise up to that point. ...

'In the meantime, our bombs began to hit home. I levelled off at masthead height, picked the widest opening in their screen and dropped to deck level, figuring any anti-aircraft fire aimed at me would also be aimed at their own ships. All their ships' fire must have been pretty busy because I was well through the screen before I noted bursting shells creeping up behind. With the throttle practically pushed through the instrument panel, I was fortunate in avoiding a contact with death by slight changes of altitude and varying the getaway course to right and left.'[19]

In the picture on the opposite page, Ordnancemen of VS-6 are pictured loading a 500lb bomb on a Douglas SBD-2 Dauntless on the flight deck of the USS Enterprise. (USNHHC)

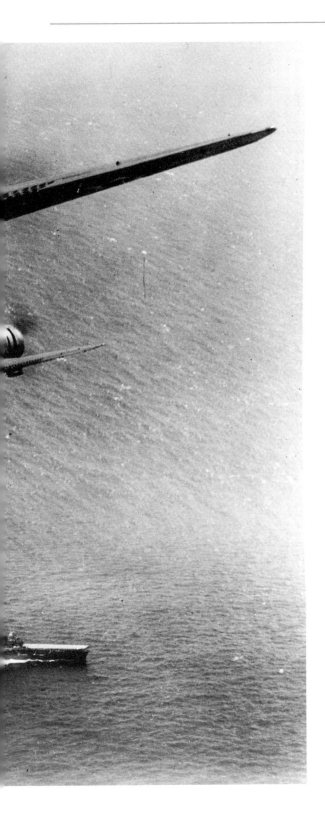

Left: The pilot of one of those Dauntless bombers from *Enterprise*'s Air Group was Norman J. Kleiss of VS-6: 'We went into echelon formation. [Lieutenant Scott] McClusky and his two wing men dived first, then [Lieutenant Wilmer Earl] Gallaher and two wingmen, then me and then the rest of Scouting Six, all heading for the *Kaga*. [Lieutenant] Dick Best and Bombing Six dived for the *Akagi*.

The *Yorktown* dive bombers dived for the *Soryu*.

'The situation was a carrier pilot's dream. No anti-aircraft, all three carriers heading straight into the wind. Two fighters were above us, but they were not making an attack. McClusky and his two wingmen missed. Earl Gallaher's 500-pound bomb hit squarely on a plane starting its take-off. His two 100-pound incendiaries hit just beside it. Immediately the whole pack of planes at the stern were in flames 50 feet high.

'I couldn't see the bombs landing from the next two planes, but flames had spread to the middle of the ship. My bombs landed exactly on the big red circle forward of the bridge. Seconds later the flames were 100 feet high. [Historian] Walter Lord later learned from the Japanese that my bomb splashed a gasoline cart, throwing its flaming contents into the *Kaga*'s bridge.

'A fighter attacked us as I pulled out of my dive. John Snowden, my gunner, disposed of him in five seconds. A second fighter came at us. John disposed of him. Then it was a survival to escape anti-aircraft fire while passing near a dozen ships until I'd reached ten miles toward Midway.

'Ten minutes after the attack I saw a large explosion amidship on the *Kaga*. Rockets of flame, pieces of steel bolted upward to about three or four thousand feet high. Dick Best's squadron had bombed the *Kaga* and the *Yorktown* bombers hit the *Soryu*. Both were burning fiercely. **>>>**

'The *Kaga* then sent up a huge brown cloud of smoke. I could no longer see the ship and presumed it was sunk. The other two fires were visible 30 miles away. As directed, I headed 40 miles toward Midway before heading to our carrier.'

Norman Kleiss was wrong in his assumption that *Kaga* had sunk. Nine bombs were aimed at *Kaga*. Her Captain, Jisaku Okada, manoeuvred his ship skilfully and the first three missed but four of the next six hit the carrier. The third bomb that hit almost completely destroyed the bridge, killing everyone there including Captain Okada. Fires were started which spread along the ship and despite the efforts of the crew it was clearly obvious that the carrier was doomed.

Only three bombs hit *Akagi*, none of which should have proven fatal but caught as she was with aircraft on deck full of fuel preparing for the upcoming strike, the fires caused by the bombs completely engulfed the entire hangar area and set off explosions which caused the fires to spread rapidly. Her fate was also sealed.

Shown on the previous pages are Douglas SBD-2 Dauntless scout bombers of VS-6, from *Enterprise*, in October 1941. (USNHHC)

Right: At least two other US airmen are known to have suffered the same fate as Ensign Wesley Osmus during the Battle of Midway.

Both men were in the crew of the VS-6 Dauntless flown by Ensign Frank Woodrow O'Flaherty – pictured here, like Osmus, prior to enlisting in the US Navy. O'Flaherty's radioman-gunner was Aviation Machinist's Mate Bruno Gaido. After their aircraft was shot down, both men were were spotted and plucked from the sea by the crew of the destroyer *Makigumo* (though some sources state it was the cruiser *Nagara*). After interrogation, O'Flaherty and Gaido were bound with ropes, tied to weighted fuel cans, and then thrown overboard to drown. (USNHHC)

10.25 hours   VB-3 Attacks the Carriers

One of those who attacked *Akagi* in one of VB-3's Douglas Dauntlesses, that coded 'B-10', was Lieutenant Harold S. Bottomley, Jr., along with his radioman-gunner AMM2c Daniel F. Johnson. 'I was scared to death!' admitted Bottomley. 'We were at about 14,000 feet, climbing in formation, making our approach toward high-speed wakes, which gradually grew into a vast armada of carriers, battleships, cruisers and then destroyers across the horizon. The cold of the cockpit at that altitude was compounded by shivers of dread and anticipation that ran up and down my spine and made my teeth chatter.'

Aiming at *Akagi*, Bottomley saw the carrier's flight deck crammed with aircraft and on a steady course into windward preparing to launch its machines. Bottomley's dive bomber was the fourth in line. He saw the Dauntless ahead of him drop a bomb which exploded directly on the forward elevator and a plane

taking off was 'flipped' like a matchstick. 'I glance again at the altimeter passing through 3,000 feet, then back to the sight and press the bomb release button switch, then reach and pull the manual toggle. I know I can't miss!'[20] Indeed, Bottomley did not miss.

Watching in disbelief as the American bombers sped towards *Akagi* was Captain Mitsuo Fuchida: 'The terrifying scream of the dive-bombers reached me first, followed by the crashing explosion of a direct hit. There was a blinding flash and then a second explosion, much louder than the first … Looking about, I was horrified at the destruction that had been wrought in a matter of seconds. There was a huge hole in the flight deck just behind the amidship elevator. The elevator itself, twisted like molten glass, was dropping into the hangar. Deck plates reeled upwards in grotesque configurations, planes stood tail up, belching livid flame and jet-black smoke.'[21]

The fires quickly spread and ignited fuel and ammunition stores which exploded, shaking the ship from bow to stern and filling the air with deadly metal splinters. The fire continued to rush along the flight deck engulfing the aircraft and detonating their torpedoes. In the course of just five minutes *Akagi* had been turned into a raging inferno.

The photograph above is of Bottomley and Johnson in the very same Dauntless they attacked *Akagi* with, pictured after the battle. However, as can be seen it is coded differently. (US National Museum of Naval Aviation)

10.29 hours   **USS *Nautilus* Spots *Soryu***
Worse was to come for Admiral Nagumo, for as soon as the Japanese Striking Force had been spotted by the Catalinas, the American submarines were directed to the enemy's location. The nine submarines moved off quickly, with USS *Grouper* being the first to make visual contact. *Grouper*, though, could not risk closing in upon the enemy as the Japanese warships were under bomb and torpedo attack. Then, at 10.29 hours, USS *Nautilus* sighted columns of smoke on the horizon, coming from the enemy carriers which had just been dive-bombed by the carrier groups, and she moved in for the attack. *Nautilus* is shown here in August 1943. (NARA)

10.45 hours   ***Soryu* Abandoned**

Soryu had received three direct hits from 1,000lb bombs. One of these penetrated to the lower hangar deck amidships, whilst the other two exploded in the upper hangar deck fore and aft. As with the other Japanese carriers, the hangars contained armed and fuelled aircraft, resulting in secondary explosions which ruptured the steam pipes in the boiler rooms. Within a very short time the fires on the ship were out of control. At 10.40 hours she stopped; her crew was ordered to abandon ship five minutes later. The destroyers *Isokaze* and *Hamakaze* rescued the survivors.

    This diorama (above) by Norman Bel Geddes, though based on incomplete wartime accounts, depicts the attack by the American dive bombers on the Japanese aircraft carriers *Akagi*, *Kaga* and *Soryu* in the morning of 4 June 1942. This angle of view depicts *Soryu* (attacked by *Yorktown* aircraft) in the middle distance, with *Kaga* and *Akagi* (both attacked by *Enterprise* aircraft) as the closer two burning ships. (USNHHC)

10.50 hours, 4 June   **The Japanese Counter-Attack**

With *Akagi*'s communications knocked out, Vice-Admiral Nagumo transferred his flag to *Nowaki* and then to the light cruiser *Nagara*, seen opposite cruising in Japanese waters. All, though, was not lost. There was still a chance of inflicting a severe blow upon the Americans and at 10.50 hours Nagumo ordered the aircraft of the only carrier that had not been hit, *Hiryu*, to counterattack. (USNHHC)

Chapter 4

THE JAPANESE HIT YORKTOWN

4 June 1942

10.54 hours   ***Hiryu*'s Bombers Set Off**
Rear Admiral Tamon Yamaguchi, commander of the Japanese Second Carrier Division on his flagship *Hiryu*, responded to Nagumo's order, announcing at 10.54 hours that: 'All our planes are taking off now for the purpose of destroying the enemy carriers.' The undamaged *Hiryu* was able to launch eighteen Aichi D3A Type 99 Carrier Bombers escorted by six Zeros to attack *Yorktown*.

The photograph below shows *Hiryu* shortly after she was completed in 1939. (Kure Maritime Museum)

Opposite: At about the same time that the aircraft on *Hiryu* were setting out to attack the US forces, this Douglas SBD-3 Dauntless scout bomber (Bureau Number 4542), of *Enterprise*'s VB-6 made an emergency landing on USS *Yorktown* at 11.40 hours on 4 June 1942. This plane, damaged during the attack on *Kaga*, put down on *Yorktown* as it was low on fuel. It was later lost with the carrier. Its crew, Ensign George Hale Goldsmith, pilot, and Radioman 1st Class James W. Patterson, Jr., can still be seen in the cockpit. Note the extensive damage to the tail. (USNHHC)

concentrated anti-aircraft barrage and powerful fighter opposition, Ensign Goldsmith, with bold determination and courageous zeal, led his squadron in dive-bombing assaults against Japanese naval units. Flying at a distance from his own forces which rendered return unlikely because of probable fuel exhaustion, he pressed home his attacks with extreme disregard for his own personal safety. His gallant intrepidity and loyal devotion to duty contributed greatly to the success of our forces and were in keeping with the highest traditions of the United States Naval Service.' (USNHHC)

Above: Another view of Ensign George H. Goldsmith's Dauntless 4542 on the deck of *Yorktown* after its emergency landing. For his actions at Midway, Goldsmith was awarded the Navy Cross, the citation of which includes the following: 'Defying extreme danger from

Below: A Douglas SBD-3 Dauntless scout bomber warming up on USS *Yorktown* in the late morning of 4 June 1942. It is Number 17 of Scouting Squadron Five (the temporarily re-designated Bombing Squadron Five), piloted by Ensign Leif Larsen, but was apparently not one of ten VS-5 planes launched on a scouting

mission shortly before noon on 4 June. Another of the squadron's SBDs succeeded in locating *Hiryu*, the only Japanese aircraft carrier of the Midway striking force that was still operational. The next aircraft, at right, is VS-5's Number 4, which did fly the scouting mission, piloted by Lieutenant John Nielsen. (NARA)

Top right: Almost immediately after *Yorktown's* Dauntless scout bombers had taken to the skies, at 11.59 hours (some sources say 11.52 hours) the carrier's radar detected aircraft from *Hiryu* approaching from the west, thirty-two miles away. In the coming force was described as 'a large number of planes, estimated at 30 or 40, on bearing 250° at a distance of 46 miles. There seemed to be 5 groups, apparently climbing as they approached.' Pictured on 4 June 1942, this is *Yorktown's* CXAM radar antenna mounted on the carrier's foretop, though the antenna and its supporting yoke are somewhat obscured by the upper structure of the foretop, the topmast, the mast's yard (with a ladder hanging from it and signal balls on two of its halliards) and the US Ensign flying from the mast. (USNHHC)

Right: At the same moment that the approaching Japanese bombers were detected, refuelling operations on *Yorktown* were immediately suspended. The sixteen VSB aircraft which had recently returned from attacking the Japanese carriers and were still in the landing circle were ordered to clear the ship. Fuel lines were drained and CO_2 introduced under pressure. An auxiliary fuel tank on the stern was dropped overboard to reduce the fire risk. All of the fighters were ordered into the air to intercept the attackers. Pictured here in the cockpit of his F4F Wildcat is Lieutenant Commander John S. Thach, VF-3's Commanding Officer. The Japanese flags on the fuselage below the canopy denote kills Thach made while flying from USS *Lexington* on 20 February 1942. (USNHHC)

Opposite page top: The Grumman F4F Wildcat seen here, at Naval Air Station Kaneohe, Oahu, on 29 May 1942, with groundcrew folding the starboard wing, was that flown by Lieutenant Commander John S. Thach, VF-3's Commanding Officer, during the afternoon combat air patrol defending USS *Yorktown*. Thach probably shot down Lieutenant Joichi Tomonaga, leader of the attacking Japanese torpedo planes, which followed the bombers, as we shall shortly see. During the early 1940s Thach developed the fighter combat technique that came to be known as the 'Thach Weave', a tactic that enabled the US fighters of the day to hold their own against the Japanese Zero. Thach used this technique in combat for the first time on 4 June 1942. (USNHHC)

Opposite page bottom: A Grumman F4F-3 Wildcat of VF-3 about to take-off. The pilot is probably Lieutenant Commander John S. Thach, and the image was taken on USS *Saratoga* a few months before Midway. Returning to the events of 4 June 1942, as *Yorktown*'s fighters raced to intercept the incoming Japanese aircraft, at a distance of fifteen to twenty miles from the carrier they intercepted about eighteen single-engine Bakugeki Type 99 Navy dive bombers and eighteen escorting fighters at 8,000-10,000 feet. So effective were the US fighters that only seven or eight bombers broke through to meet the formidable screen of anti-aircraft fire thrown up by the US warships. (USNHHC)

12.10 hours   **_Yorktown_ Hit**

Within moments, the bombers that had broken through *Yorktown*'s fighters were bearing down on the carrier and its escorts – she was accompanied by two cruisers and five destroyers. As a result of the small number of attackers, the naval gunners selected individual targets as opposed to laying a barrage. The anti-aircraft guns opened fire at 12.06 hours a range of 9,000 yards. An official history takes up the story:

'One plane was shot down soon after coming within range. As the next plane came in and dove to its bomb release point it was cut to pieces by antiaircraft fire, but its bomb tumbled on the *Yorktown*'s deck just abaft the number two elevator. The third plane dove and

was hit at the instant its pilot released his bomb, which fell so close astern that fragments wounded gunners on the fantail and started small fires, while pieces of the plane fell in the Yorktown's wake. Three planes dove from the port beam and released their bombs before our gunners found them. Two bombs were misses, one wide and one close to starboard, but the third hit the deck on the starboard side and penetrated the uptakes, where it exploded. The plane which dropped it crashed into the sea beside the ship. A seventh plane circled and dove from ahead. The bomb, dropped an instant before the plane was shot down, hit the number one elevator and exploded above the fourth deck, starting a fire. The last plane missed on the starboard beam.'

The photograph on the previous page shows USS Yorktown under attack by dive bombers from Hiryu just after midday on 4 June 1942, as seen from USS Astoria. One Aichi Type 99 carrier bomber is falling ahead of the ship, with its tail shot off. A bomb has just hit a few hundred feet astern. (NARA)

Above: The view from the cruiser USS Portland as Yorktown comes under attack by Japanese dive bombers shortly after noon on 4 June 1942. She has been hit just aft of the midships elevator, with white smoke visible streaming from that area. This bomb exploded on the flight deck, causing many casualties in the vicinity. It also started fires in the hangar below. The objects in the foreground are the wing and tail of two of Portland's floatplanes. (USNHHC)

Opposite: One of the bombs dropped by the Japanese bombers, from an aircraft which had been shot to pieces by anti-aircraft fire, fell and exploded on the flight deck. Here we see hurried repairs to the hole that the bomb made. This hole, about twelve feet in diameter, was caused as the 250-kilogram bomb exploded on contact with the flight deck. Its explosion killed and injured many men on nearby guns and set fires on the hangar deck. Two of the dead are lying covered over in the top centre, by a battery of .50 calibre machine-guns. The photograph was taken looking aft and slightly to starboard from the rear edge of the midships' aircraft elevator. The hole was quickly repaired with a timber and steel plate cover, allowing resumption of flight deck activities. This hole, minus the repair, was clearly visible when Yorktown's wreck was examined in May 1998. (USNHHC)

Left: Corpsmen treating casualties on USS *Yorktown* after the carrier had been hit by the bombs at about midday on 4 June 1942. The dead and wounded were members of the crew of the anti-aircraft gun position that can be seen in the centre background.

They were struck by fragments from a bomb that exploded on the flight deck just aft of the midships elevator. This view looks directly to starboard from the front of the midships elevator. (NARA)

Below: It is generally stated that none of the bombers that first attacked *Yorktown* survived, though some reports suggest one might have slipped away.

This is a portrait of Lieutenant Michio Kobayashi who was killed leading the bombing attack on *Yorktown*. As stated earlier, it is likely that it was Lieutenant Commander John S. Thach who shot down Kobayashi's aircraft. (USNHHC)

Above: Firefighters at work in *Yorktown*'s hangar, soon after midday, extinguishing fires caused by the bomb that detonated on the flight deck just aft of the midships' elevator. (USNHHC)

Left: Though a rather fuzzy time exposure image, this photograph shows the scene inside *Yorktown*'s hangar shortly after the fires had been extinguished. It was taken looking directly aft, with the sloping inner uptake sides at left. One bomb, which detonated on the flight deck just aft of the midships aircraft elevator, set fires in the area seen in the left distance. (USNHHC)

Opposite: Another of the bombs that struck *Yorktown* punctured her uptakes and knocked out the boilers, causing her to lose power and come to a dead halt in the water. The dense smoke that can be seen here is coming from the uptakes. (USNHHC)

Above: With *Yorktown* severely damaged, Rear Admiral Fletcher transferred his flag to the cruiser USS *Aatoria*.

In this photograph, taken at about 13.00 hours, the cruiser's No.2 Motor Whaleboat is alongside and Captain Spencer S. Lewis, Fletcher's Chief of Staff, is just starting up the ladder to board *Astoria*. Fletcher is behind him, just to the right of the boat's centerline, wearing binoculars with white straps. Commander Chauncey Crutcher, *Astoria*'s Executive Officer, is watching at upper left. (USNHHC)

Opposite page: Bomb fragment damage in *Yorktown*'s hangar. This damage was caused by the bomb that detonated on the flight deck just aft of the midships elevator, sending fragments into the hangar and setting fires that were quickly extinguished. Note the water on the deck, as well as the ordnance carts and chain fall mechanism stowed in the area. (NARA)

Opposite: Though the frantic engagement with the Japanese bombers was over by 12.15 hours, three hits had been made on *Yorktown*. This is a view of the upper after end of *Yorktown*'s island taken during the attacks on 4 June. (USNHHC)

Above: USS *Astoria*, in the background, steams by *Yorktown* shortly after the carrier had been hit by the three Japanese bombs. The dense smoke is from fires in *Yorktown*'s uptakes. The image was taken by Photographer 2nd Class William G. Roy, from the starboard side of *Yorktown*'s flight deck, just in front of the forward 5"/38 gun gallery.

Both guns are manned and ready. Projecting bars beyond the gun barrels are aircraft parking outriggers. Note open sights on the guns and splinter shield plates, fastened together with bolts.

Repairs to the carrier were quickly completed. Indeed, the hole in the flight deck had been covered over in less than half an hour. By 13.40 hours, repairs to the uptakes permitted the other boilers to be cut in, except for Nos. 2 and 3, which were disabled. By 13.50 hours, *Yorktown* was able to proceed at about 20 knots, and fires were sufficiently under control to permit refuelling of fighters on deck. (USNHHC)

Above: Despite Lieutenant McClusky's hope that *Hornet*'s Air Group would follow, none of Scouting Eight or Bomber Eight was able to locate Nagumo's Striking Force, emphasising the importance of McClusky's actions which led to the discovery of the Japanese carriers. At 13.20 hours *Hornet* began recovering its aircraft, which returned in groups, large and small, with one section of Bombing Eight returning alone.

Thirteen planes of VB-8 landed at Midway due to lack of fuel after having searched for the Japanese ships beyond their allowable range. Two of these ran out of fuel completely and landed in the lagoon at Midway.

None of Fighting Eight which went with the attack group returned to the ship. They remained with Scouting and Bombing Eight until forced to head for Midway, also due to

lack of fuel. Here a Douglas SBD-3 Dauntless of VB-8 is pictured landing on *Hornet* during the battle. Note how close the aircraft is to the LSO, or Landing Signal Officer, who is crouching on the right-hand corner of the flight deck. (US National Museum of Naval Aviation)

Above: Two SBD-3 scout bombers fly near USS *Yorktown* at about 13.30 hours on 4 June.

The carrier is still dead in the water and unable to recover aircraft.

These two planes are probably those piloted by VB-3's Commanding Officer, Lieutenant Commander Maxwell F. Leslie, and Lieutenant (Junior Grade) Paul A. Holmberg, who were returning from attacking the Japanese carrier *Soryu*. Low on fuel, both ditched nearby and their crews were recovered safely. (USNHHC)

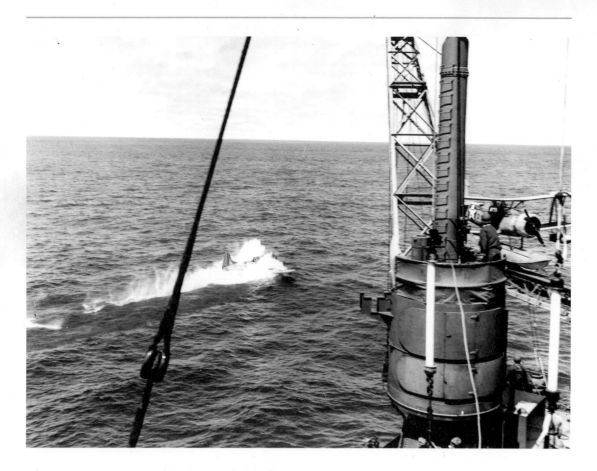

Above: An SBD-3 scout bomber, probably flown by the Commanding Officer of VB-3, Lieutenant Commander Maxwell F. Leslie, ditches alongside USS *Astoria* at 13.48 hours on 4 June 1942. This was one of two VB-3 planes that ditched near *Astoria* after they were unable to land on the damaged USS *Yorktown*. This photograph was taken from atop *Astoria*'s aft superstructure; note her port aircraft crane and the floatplane on her port catapult. (USNHHC)

Above: A photograph taken looking astern on USS *Pensacola* as she steams to the aid of USS *Yorktown* during the early afternoon of 4 June 1942. The warships following are probably USS *Benham*, on the left, and USS *Vincennes*. It is believed that the USS *Balch* is out of view to the right. These four ships were detached from Task Force 16 to augment the screen of the nearby Task Force 17 after *Yorktown* was hit and temporarily stopped by Japanese dive bombers.

Below: Just visible towards the centre above the horizon is another view of one of the two Dauntlesses of VB-3 which ditched alongside *Astoria* after running out of fuel when unable to land on *Yorktown*. The second of the two SBD-3 planes was piloted by Lieutenant (Junior Grade) Paul A. Holmberg. This photograph was taken from USS *Pensacola*. (USNHHC)

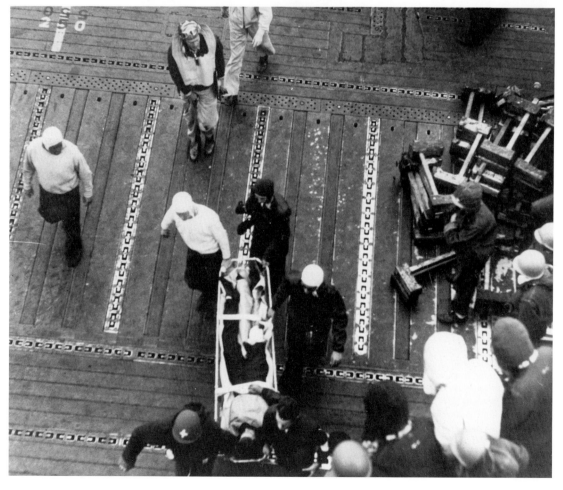

Opposite top and bottom: One Dauntless of VB-3, that piloted by Ensign Bunyan R. Cooner, landed on USS *Enterprise*.

Here we see one of Cooner's crew, Aviation Ordnanceman 2nd Class Clifton R. Bassett, who was wounded during the attack upon *Hiryu*, being carried from the carrier's flight deck. Bunyan was the aircraft's radioman/gunner. Cooner can be seen in both images wearing the flying helmet and life preserver. (USNHHC)

Below: As the American submarine USS *Nautilus* approached the Japanese carriers, she encountered what was believed to be *Soryu*, now on even keel with the hull apparently undamaged. Whilst the carrier was smoking, there were no flames and the fires seemed under control.

She was also making two to three knots, accompanied by two cruisers. *Nautilus* closed to within striking range and, at 13.59 hours, fired three torpedoes. This diorama by Norman Bel Geddes depicts the attack by *Nautilus* as seen through the submarine's periscope. *Nautilus* reported she had attacked *Soryu*, and that her torpedoes had exploded when they hit the target. Most evidence, however, is that the ship attacked was *Kaga*, and that the torpedoes failed to detonate. (USNHHC)

The captain of USS *Nautilus*, Lieutenant Commander William H. Brockman, Jr., pictured after being presented with the Navy Cross, awarded for his performance during the Battle of Midway, at the awards ceremony at the Pearl Harbor submarine base, 7 November 1942. (NARA)

Chapter 5
THE TORPEDO BOMBERS STRIKE
4 June 1942

Above: USS *Yorktown* photographed after being hit by Japanese bombs just after midday on 4 June 1942. This view was taken shortly after the ship lost power. Note the F4F-4 fighters are still spotted forward, their location during the attack. (USNHHC)

USS *Yorktown* pictured from USS *Astoria* after the carrier was hit by Japanese bombs shortly after midday on 4 June. Fires are still burning in her uptakes, whilst damage repair parties are working on the flight deck to cover bomb entry holes in the forward elevator and alongside the island, as well as a large bomb hole just aft of the midships elevator.

Note the floatplane on *Astoria*'s starboard catapult. (USNHHC)

Left: Surrounded by her escorts, after being hit by Japanese bombs shortly after midday, this photograph of *Yorktown* was taken after the flight deck repairs had progressed far enough to allow the repositioning of aircraft. (USNHHC)

Main image: The fires on USS *Yorktown* grow in intensity as the carrier still lies dead in the water after being hit by Japanese bombs on 4 June. By the time this picture was taken, the F4F-4 fighters that had been parked at the forward end of the flight deck during the attack had been repositioned aft in the take-off position. Two SBD-3 scout bombers can also be seen through the open sides of her after hangar bay.

Left: Another view of USS *Yorktown* afire and dead in the water that was taken roughly an hour after the dive bombers struck just after midday. The photographer was on USS *Pensacola*, whilst the larger ship to the left of *Yorktown* is USS *Portland*. Though the bombers had departed, *Yorktown*'s onslaught was far from over for, at 13.31 hours, *Hiryu* ordered its torpedo bombers against the US carrier. (USNHHC)

Below: At 14.27 hours, *Pensacola*, which had assumed radar guard after the *Yorktown* was damaged, picked up enemy planes bearing 340° at a distance of thirty-three miles. A combat air patrol of six of *Yorktown*'s fighters, which had rearmed and refuelled on board *Enterprise*, was already airborne. Four of these were vectored out to intercept the enemy, and in a few seconds the other two followed. The first four, flying at 10,000 to 12,000 feet, overran the enemy planes, which were coming in at 5,000 feet, and had to turn back to find them. The other two met the Japanese ten to fourteen miles out.

On *Yorktown*, all refuelling was suspended, and CO_2 once again introduced into the fuel system. Of the ten fighters on deck, eight had sufficient fuel reserves to go into action. The fourth of these was being launched when *Yorktown*'s port battery opened fire; the vessels to starboard of *Yorktown* had to hold their fire until the fighters had cleared the area.

When the US fighters engaged the Japanese attackers, they managed to shoot down between five and seven of the torpedo planes before the warships opened fire. About eight attackers continued to press on with their mission, some of which are pictured here, from *Pensacola*, flying through a fierce anti-aircraft barrage while closing on *Yorktown* to deliver their torpedoes. (USNHHC)

Opposite page top: As one official US history notes, 'the curtain of fire thrown up by our ships was so heavy that it seemed impossible for a plane to pass through it and survive. Indeed, according to some reports, a few enemy planes circled outside, not daring to come in. Seven or eight, however, came through.'[23] This image captured the moment that a Japanese Type 97 Nakajima B5N shipboard attack aircraft (upper right) approached *Yorktown* during the mid-afternoon torpedo attack by *Hiryu*'s force on 4 June 1942. Taken from above *Yorktown*'s signal station, immediately aft of her tripod foremast, the photographer was looking forward and to starboard. (USNHHC)

Opposite page bottom: Photographed from USS *Pensacola*, Japanese Nakajima Type 97 shipboard attack aircraft from the carrier *Hiryu* battle through anti-aircraft shell bursts while running in towards USS *Yorktown* to deliver a torpedo attack during the mid-afternoon of 4 June. At least four Japanese aircraft are visible in this image.

Though the Japanese reported that all nine of its planes dropped their Type 91 aerial torpedoes, only four were seen to enter the water. *Yorktown* avoided two torpedoes which crossed her bow, but the last two, released at about 800 yards struck her on the port side amidships, the first at 14.45 hours and the second thirty seconds later. (USNHHC)

Above: Seen from USS Pensacola, one of *Hiryu*'s Type 97 shipboard attack aircraft (far right) approach the drop point during the torpedo attack on USS *Yorktown* in the mid-afternoon of 4 June. The plane's Type 91 torpedo is just visible below the fuselage. Note the anti-aircraft fire, with shell fragments splashing in the water below the bursts. (NARA)

Opposite page: A Japanese Type 97 crashes while attempting to deliver a torpedo attack on *Yorktown*. The small object just to left of the camera aiming cross, behind the shell burst, appears to be a Grumman F4F-4 Wildcat fighter banking away. (USNHHC)

Above: A fatal hit for USS *Yorktown*. Also taken from *Pensacola*, this image captures the very moment that *Yorktown* heels over as the second torpedo strikes her amidships. (USNHHC)

Above: Two of the Japanese torpedo bombers fly past *Yorktown* after dropping their torpedoes. (USNHHC)

Right: The US history continues its narrative: 'As they passed our screening vessels our gunners followed them even though our own ships lay beyond in the line of fire. It seems that only four or five survived long enough to drop their torpedoes.

'Two of these the *Yorktown* avoided by skilful maneuvering [*sic*], so that they passed under her bow. Two others, however, could not be avoided, and they caught her admidships on the port side. The two explosions at 1445 were about 30 seconds apart. The planes which scored these hits

were shot down either in passing the *Yorktown* or in attempting to pass through the fire of her escorting vessels. It is believed that not one of the attacking squadron returned to its carrier.'[24] (USNHHC)

Above: By 14.47 hours, the firing had ceased. *Yorktown*, however, was clearly in trouble and could be seen listing heavily to port whilst losing speed and turning in a small circle to port. The carrier soon stopped and white smoke poured from her stacks. (USNHHC)

Left: Lieutenant Joichi Tomonaga was *Hiryu*'s Air Group Commander who led the torpedo raid on *Yorktown*. Like Lieutenant Kobayashi, he did not survive the attack. (USNHHC)

111

Above: The stricken USS *Yorktown* pictured dead in the water and listing heavily. The section of catwalk jutting above the flight deck, port side amidships, is directly above the place where the torpedoes struck the ship's hull. (USNHHC)

Below: Though it appears to have suffered from partial double-exposure, this picture was taken looking to port, amidships, on the flight deck of USS *Yorktown* shortly after the carrier was hit by two Japanese aerial torpedoes, 4 June 1942. The damaged port side catwalk, which was broken and bent upwards by the explosion of an aerial torpedo on the hull below, can clearly be seen. Arresting gear wire can also be seen. (USNHHC)

Above: Inside *Yorktown* all of the lights had gone out. The diesel generators cut in, but the circuit breakers would not hold and the ship remained in darkness. The list gradually increased to 26°. Without power nothing could be done to correct the situation. The Commanding Officer and the Damage Control Officer thought it probable that USS *Yorktown* would capsize in a few minutes. Consequently, at 14.55 hours the order was given to abandon ship.

This is the scene on *Yorktown*'s flight deck, with men balancing themselves on the listing deck and lifejackets being worn as the crew prepare to abandon ship.

The F4F-4 Wildcat visible in the background is VF-3 No.6 (Bureau Number 5165), which had been flown by Ensign Brainard T. Macomber during the morning attacks on the Japanese carrier fleet. Insufficient fuel prevented it from being launched to defend *Yorktown*. (USNHHC)

Above: *Yorktown* being abandoned by her crew after she was hit by the torpedoes, 4 June. USS *Balch* is standing by at right. Note the oil slick surrounding the damaged carrier, and inflatable life raft being deployed off her stern. (USNHHC)

Opposite: A distant view of *Yorktown* being abandoned, with a destroyer standing by off the listing carrier's stern, whilst the USS *Vincennes* steams by in the middle distance. (USNHHC)

Below: A number of destroyers stand by to pick up survivors as USS *Yorktown* is abandoned during the afternoon of 4 June, as seen from USS Pensacola. They are, left to right, USS *Benham*, USS *Russell*, USS Balch, and, at right, USS *Anderson*. Note the survivors climbing down the carrier's hull. (USNHHC)

Above: As well as the drama being played out around USS *Yorktown*, the Japanese carrier *Kaga* was still riddled with fires that were burning out of control. At 16.40 hours, its crew was also instructed to abandon ship. Here is a photograph of *Kaga* taken before the war.

Below: Revenge for *Yorktown* was not long in coming. At 15.30 hours, *Enterprise* began launching an attack group of eleven of her own scout bombers and fourteen that had transferred from *Yorktown* in a bid to eliminate

the only sole Japanese carrier capable of offensive action, *Hiryu*. Eleven of these were armed with one 1,000lb bomb each and thirteen with a single 500lb bomb. *Hornet* launched a squadron of sixteen scout bombers at 16.03 hours.

The bombers spotted the enemy at 16.50 hours and launched their attack at 17.05 hours, diving down out of the sun from 19,000 feet. They were engaged by fighters from *Hiryu* which shot down one of the bombers before it began its dive and another two as they pulled

away after unleashing their bombs. Nevertheless, four bombs struck the Japanese carrier, rendering *Hiryu* a mass of flames. One of the bombers targeted a battleship, presumed to be *Haruna*, but without success.

By the time *Hornet*'s bombers arrived, at 17.30 hours, *Hiryu* was burning so fiercely it was obviously unnecessary to damage her any further, and the American airman switched their attention to what they believed were a battleship and a cruiser, but were, in all probability, the cruisier *Tone*, which reported

that ten bombs had been directed towards it, and another cruiser *Chikuma*, which declared five bombs. Neither warships, however, suffered any damage.

Here USS *Hornet* is seen in the South Pacific before the Battle of Midway. (NARA)

Above: *Yorktown* lists heavily after she was abandoned during the afternoon of 4 June 1942. A pair of F4F-4 Wildcat fighters are still parked on her flight deck, aft of the island. (USNHHC)

Above: The rescue of *Yorktown*'s survivors underway at 19.00 hours on 4 June 1942. This picture depicts the destroyer USS *Benham*, with 720 survivors on board, closing with the cruiser USS *Portland*. A report of unidentified aircraft caused *Benham* to break away before transferring any of the survivors to the cruiser and they remained on board her until the following morning. The listing *Yorktown* is in the right distance.

Thirteen minutes after this photograph was taken, with fires still burning throughout the ship, the carrier *Soryu* slipped beneath the waves. Then, after Nagumo had moved his flag from *Akagi*, orders were given to flood that carrier's magazines, but the pump system failed. With no hope of saving her, the crew abandoned ship at 19.25 hours, the men being taken off by the destroyers *Arashi* and *Nowake*. (USNHHC)

Chapter 6

OPERATION MI CANCELLED

5 June 1942

Above: As darkness fell on the evening of 4 June both sides took advantage of the relative calm to treat the wounded, repair damaged warships, and assess the cost of the day's engagements. The same was the case on land. Here, oil tanks can be seen burning on Sand Island, Midway, during the night of 4-5 June 1942, having been set on fire in the morning attack of 4 June. This view looks roughly southwest along what was then Sand Island's southern shore.

Throughout the late hours of the fourth there were a few isolated engagements. The light from this fire guided at least one Marine aviator back to Midway after an attempted night attack mission against Japanese ships. Likewise, six B-17s attacked a burning carrier and other Japanese ships at about 18.30 hours, encountering several Zeros in the process. The possibility that a fifth Japanese carrier was operating in the vicinity could still not be discounted. Neither was it certain that the loss of air support would deter the Japanese from attempting a landing on Midway. Indeed, there were indications that they were still en route to undertake such an attack.

At 21.15 hours on the 4th, the US submarines were ordered to form on a circle at radius 100 miles from Midway. (USNHHC)

02.15 hours — *Mogami* and *Mikuma* Collide

Despite the obvious successes of the previous day, the situation remained very unclear on the morning of the 5th. Fletcher, having abandoned his flagship, *Yorktown*, handed over control of the operation to Admiral Spruance. Then, at about 02.15 hours the submarine USS *Tambor*, seen here running on the surface, reported spotting numerous unidentified enemy ships just ninety miles away to the west.

The Japanese had certainly not given up all hope of inflicting crippling damage upon the US warships. Though the sighting of the *Tambor* had caused Vice Admiral Kondo to stop his transports moving on Midway, he still hoped that the powerful Japanese surface craft could achieve the victory the Japanese sought.

He sent a signal to Nagumo to that effect, but the commander of the Striking Force knew how severely his ships had been hit, and he ignored Kondo. That was until he received a message from Yamamoto that Nagumo was to combine with Kondo and to press on with the operation as planned. That order, though, would soon be rescinded.

At the sight of *Tambor* the surface cruiser *Mogami* was ordered to take evasive action. Turning hard to port, *Mogami* miscalculated the distance between her and her sister ship *Mikuma*. *Mogami* rammed *Mikuma*, tearing a hole in its fuel tank as well as ripping forty feet off her own bow.

After a short while *Mogami* was able to continue but could only make twelve knots. Vice Admiral Takeo Kurita, in command of the support group on board *Kumano*, could not endanger the other two undamaged cruisers under his command and he left *Mogami* with *Mikuma* and sped away with *Kumano* and *Suzuya*.

This was the final, crushing blow to Yamamoto's hopes and Operation MI was cancelled at 05.55 hours. (USNHHC)

Above: The burning Japanese aircraft carrier *Hiryu* photographed by a plane from the carrier *Hōshō* shortly after sunrise on 5 June 1942. This aircraft was crewed by pilot Shigeo Nakamura and his observer, Kiyoshi Ōniwa, Throughout the night every effort had been made by *Hiryu*'s crew to escape from the American task forces and to bring the fires under control but without success. One by one, the men in the carrier's engine rooms died at their posts. Eventually *Hiryu* took on a 15-degree list. At 03.15 hours on the 5th it was reluctantly accepted that the carrier would have to be abandoned. Once the order was given, the crew was taken off by the destroyers *Kazegumo* and *Makigumo*. (USNHHC)

Right: The view from the bridge of the Japanese cruiser *Mogami* over her badly damaged bow whilst being refuelled by the tanker *Nichiei Maru* after the Battle of Midway. Note the Japanese flag on the forward turret as for aerial recognition.

Above: Another photograph of *Hiryu* burning, shortly after sunrise on 5 June, taken from the aircraft from *Hōshō*. Note the collapsed flight deck at right. Part of the forward elevator is standing upright just in front of the island, where it had been thrown by an explosion in the hangar. (USNHHC)

Below: The Japanese light carrier *Hōshō* was with Yamamoto's Main Force and too far away from the Carrier Striking Force to participate in the battle, but on 5 June its aircraft helped guide the remnants of Nagumo's force to a rendezvous with the Main Body. *Hōshō* is shown here in December 1942. (Kure Maritime Museum)

Above: Two men remained on *Hiryu* after the rest of the crew had been taken off – Rear Admiral Yamaguchi and the captain of the carrier Captain T. Kaki. Both men opted to remain and go down with the ship. In this Japanese painting, Yamaguchi is depicted in the middle of the scene as he bids farewell to his staff. *Hiryu* was sent to the bottom by a single torpedo from *Makigumo*. (NARA)

Left: On 5 June contact was made with the retreating Japanese forces at 05.45 hours. Forty-five minutes later the remaining Dauntlesses of VB-2, along with the Vought SB2U Vindicators of VMSB-241 led by Captain Richard Eugene Fleming, were given orders to attack what was described as a crippled battleship, but was in fact the cruiser *Mikuma*.

Flying with VB-2 was Lieutenant George E. Koutelas, seen here in this pencil drawn portrait. 'No enemy aircraft was sighted going in or out,' Koutelas later recalled. 'We climbed to four thousand feet … We attacked at 08.50. Captain Fleming was leading the attack and was hit by AA fire and went down in flames. He stayed in his dive even though he was in flames and dropped his bomb at 500 feet. He got a near miss on the stern of the ship. I was the last one of the six to dive. While I was in my dive I saw two near misses about 30 feet off the starboard bow. The two bombs were about 20 feet apart. I made my dive diagonally across the starboard bow, releasing at about 1,000 feet. After releasing I turned to 080 degrees and headed for home. While I was turning, I saw a hit about one-third the way back from the bow. The ship was listing badly and was winding up in a tight right turn.'[25] In fact, there were no hits on *Mikuma*.

For his actions at Midway, Koutelas was awarded the Navy Cross. The citation includes the following: 'During the initial attack upon an enemy aircraft carrier, Second Lieutenant Koutelas, under tremendous fire from Japanese fighter guns and anti-aircraft batteries, dived his plane to the perilously low altitude of four hundred feet before releasing his bomb. On 4 June, after less than four hours' sleep, he participated in an assault which resulted in the severe damaging of a Japanese battleship.' (USNHHC)

Right: Although *Mikuma* had not been hit in the attack by VB-2 and VMSB-241, at the time it was thought that Fleming had indeed struck the cruiser. According to Fuchida and Okumiya, 'the pilot [Fleming] after being hit by anti-aircraft fire, attempted a daring suicide crash into *Mikuma*'s bridge. He missed the bridge but crashed into the after turret, spreading fire

over the air intake of the starboard engine room.

'This caused an explosion of gas fumes below, killing all hands working in the engine room. This was a damaging blow to the cruiser, hitherto unscathed except for the slight hull damage received in the collision with *Mogami*.'[26]

However, it later transpired that this was not the case, Fleming's Vindicator crashing not into *Mikuma* but the sea. Nevertheless, for what was undoubtedly an act of great courage, Fleming was posthumously awarded the Medal of Honor, the only man to be decorated with America's highest award during the battle. His citation states the following:

'When his squadron Commander was shot down during the initial attack upon an enemy aircraft carrier, Captain Fleming led the

remainder of the division with such fearless determination that he dived his own plane to the perilously low altitude of four hundred feet before releasing his bomb. Although his craft was riddled by 179 hits in the blistering hail of fire that burst upon him from Japanese fighter guns and antiaircraft batteries, he pulled out with only two minor wounds inflicted upon himself.

'On the night of June 4, when the Squadron Commander lost his way and became separated from the others, Captain Fleming brought his own plane in for a safe landing at its base despite hazardous weather conditions and total darkness.

'The following day, after less than four hours' sleep, he led the second division of his squadron in a coordinated glide-bombing and dive-bombing assault upon a Japanese battleship [sic, the cruiser *Mikuma*]. Undeterred by a fateful approach glide, during which his ship [aircraft] was struck and set afire, he grimly pressed home his attack to an altitude of five hundred feet, released his bomb to score a near-miss on the stern of his target, then crashed to the sea in flames.'

This photograph of Richard Fleming shows him as an Aviation Cadet upon his arrival at Naval Air Station Pensacola in 1940. (US National Museum of Naval Aviation)

Below: The old battleship *Haruna*, it may be recalled, had survived two attacks on 4 June. She suffered no hits that day, and claimed to have shot down five American aircraft. On 5 June, she took on survivors from the four destroyed Japanese aircraft carriers before returning to Japan. (USNHHC)

Below: Whilst *Yorktown* had been abandoned by its crew, the carrier had stopped settling in the water with no immediate indication that she was going to sink. Captain Buckmaster saw that there was still a chance of saving the ship and the former minesweeper-turned tug USS *Vireo* was ordered out from Pearl Harbor. *Vireo*, seen here a few weeks after the Battle of Midway, arrived on the scene at 11.35 hours and by 13.08 a line had been attached to *Yorktown* and the crippled carrier was taken in tow. The tug struggled laboriously to pull the big warship along, barely able to make more than two knots, shielded by a force of destroyers. (USNHHC)

Right: Lieutenant James Claude Legg, pictured here on 2 May 1942, was the captain of USS *Vireo* during the Battle of Midway. He was awarded a Navy Cross for his endeavours. His citation details part of his actions: 'Immediately proceeding through the hazardous submarine-infested waters, Lieutenant Commander Legg sent a working party on board the crippled *Yorktown* to connect a tow wire and, working untiringly for a twenty-four hour period in a desperate attempt to tow it clear of the perilous area, expeditiously ordered the tow wire out when a vessel to the starboard side of the *Yorktown* was hit by an enemy torpedo and sunk.

Then, going to the aid of the survivors from the stricken ship, he effected their rescue and subsequently brought the *Vireo* alongside the heavily listing *Yorktown* to evacuate its Commanding Officer and the personnel on board.' (USNHHC)

Below: With the cancellation of Operation *MI* the Japanese sought to escape beyond the range of the American aircraft. On the other hand, throughout the afternoon of the 5th, Spruance tried to locate and destroy as many enemy ships as he could. The *Hornet*'s air group of twenty-six Dauntlesses searched up to a range of 315 miles without finding any Japanese vessels until, at 18.04 hours they spotted what was thought to be a light cruiser or destroyer. This was, it seems, the destroyer *Tanikaze*, which subsequently reported being attacked by twenty-six bombers, resulting in eleven near-misses, but no direct hits. *Enterprise*'s air group of thirty-six Dauntlesses also recorded an attack on what was also believed to be an unidentified cruiser or destroyer at 18.30 hours, losing one aircraft.

The US aircraft had very little fuel left after their extensive searches and one of *Hornet*'s attack group ran completely out of fuel and had to ditch near *Enterprise* in the dark. The crew were rescued by the destroyer USS *Aylwin*.

In this photograph, *Tanikaze* is shown at anchor in April 1941. (Kure Maritime Museum)

Chapter 7

LAST SHOTS

6 June 1942

Above: While Task Force 16 was pursuing the retreating Japanese ships, some 400 miles to the east the tug *Vireo*, towing *Yorktown*, was struggling to make any headway. Nevertheless, the carrier was still afloat, and it was decided to make every effort to save this valuable ship. As soon as it was light on the morning of the 6th, the destroyer USS *Hammann* transferred a salvage team of twenty-nine officers and 141 men to the carrier to work under Captain Buckmaster. In order to supply power to the submersible equipment that would pump the water out of the carrier it was found necessary to secure *Hammann* alongside. At the same time, in a bid to help the salvage operation, it was decided to lighten the listing carrier by disposing of all movable equipment. As can be seen in this photograph, this included the aircraft stranded on the ship, such as the Douglas Devastator seen here being prepared for jettisoning. This view was taken looking to port, out of the forward hangar bay opening. (USNHHC)

Above: Survivors from *Yorktown* are checked in on board USS *Fulton* having been transferred from USS *Portland* for transportation to Pearl Harbor, 6 June 1942. Note the life jackets, which appear to be oil-stained. (USNHHC)

Next page: Throughout the morning of 6 June, Spruance had received numerous reports from his scouting aircraft warning of the presence of Japanese naval units, which it was thought included two battleships. As soon as

he was certain of the enemy's position, Spruance ordered an attack, and at 08.00 hours *Hornet* began launching a powerful force of twenty-six Dauntlesses of which eighteen were armed with 1,000lb bombs, the rest 500lb bombs. They were supported by eight fighters.

The aircraft found the enemy units without difficulty, and at 09.30 hours launched their attack on what transpired not to be a battleship but the stricken *Mikuma*. They achieved three hits and two near misses. The

cruiser's steering was damaged in the attack and she was left turning to starboard in uncontrollable circles.

The aircraft then moved on to *Mogami* which was struck twice. One 1,000lb bomb landed on top of the No.5 turret, penetrated its armour and killed the entire turret's crew. The second bomb hit amidships, damaged torpedo tubes and started fires below decks. One aircraft was shot down by the anti-aircraft guns of the cruiser.

Shown above is one of the most famous photographs of the Battle of Midway, showing Dauntlesses from *Hornet* approaching the burning *Mikuma* to make the third set of attacks on her. (USNHHC)

Right: At 11.15 hours *Enterprise* launched thirty-one of its Dauntless scout bombers, each armed with 1,000lb bombs, with twelve Wildcats in support. At 12.00 hours they sighted a group of warships, believed to consist of one heavy cruiser, one light cruiser and several destroyers. While part of the bombing group searched off ahead to find the reported battleships, one squadron dived upon *Mikuma* followed by the subsequent squadrons which targeted *Mogami*.

The latter cruiser was hit again twice, once amidships and once forward of the bridge. A Douglas SBD-3 Dauntless is shown here flying over *Enterprise* later in 1942. (US National Naval Aviation Museum)

Above: This representation by Norman Bel Geddes depicts the attack by SBD dive bombers from *Hornet* and *Enterprise* on *Mogami* and *Mikuma* and two destroyers, on 6 June 1942. *Mikuma* is the ship shown trailing oil to the right. (USNHHC)

Above: The Japanese heavy cruiser *Mikuma* afire and dead in the water on 6 June 1942, as seen from an SBD dive bomber, probably from USS *Hornet*, during the day's third attack. A destroyer, either *Asashio* or *Arashio*, is nearby, attempting to recover *Mikuma*'s crew. The photograph was taken from the gunner's seat, looking aft, with the barrel of a .30 calibre machine-gun in the right foreground and the plane's vertical tail at the extreme right. (USNHHC)

Below: The bombs which hit *Mikuma* had started uncontrollable fires, leaving her dead in the water.

The destroyer *Arashio* attempted to go alongside to save the crew but the fires were too fierce and all she could do was lower her boats and pick men up out of the water.

At 13.00 hours, or thereabouts, the decision was taken to abandon the cruiser. (USNHHC)

Above: The efforts to salvage *Yorktown* continued throughout the morning. However, a reconnaissance aircraft from the cruiser *Chikuma* had spotted *Yorktown* and its location was passed onto the submarine *I-168*, which lost no time in reaching the scene of the salvage operation.

At 13.35 hours, the wakes of four torpedoes were spotted to the starboard of *Yorktown*. *Hammann* immediately went astern but she was hit by two of the torpedoes, the other two struck *Yorktown*.

On board *Hammann* was Lieutenant Charles C. Hartigan: 'The *Hammann* was moored portside to the *Yorktown*. At this time four torpedoes were reported on our starboard beam. ... Immediately following the first torpedo the second torpedo hit. ... regaining my senses ... I saw that the forecastle deck was awash. When I got down to the bridge, the executive officer was going down the vertical ladder ... the Captain was the only man on the bridge. We inspected the pilot house, chart house, and radar room and found no one. ... the captain, executive officer, engineer officer and myself all jumped into the water and swam clear of the ship. The captain pointed at a mess attendant, Raby, ... holding onto the forecastle life line. I swam back to get him ... just before I got there the ship went under. Raby ... floated free. At about this time a terrific underwater explosion went off which all but knocked me out.'[27] The explosion Hartigan refers to was one of a number which were the detonations of the destroyer's depth charges and torpedoes.

This diorama by Norman Bel Geddes illustrates the moment the Japanese submarine's torpedoes struck. (USNHHC)

Above: Another of Norman Bel Geddes' dioramas, this one depicts the explosion of the depth charges on USS *Hammann* as she sank alongside *Yorktown*. The tug *Vireo* is shown on the left, coming back to pick up survivors, as destroyers break off and fan out to search for the submarine. (USNHHC)

Right: The stern of USS *Hammann* stands upright out of the water following the torpedoing by *I-168* in the afternoon of 6 June 1942. The scene was photographed from the starboard forecastle deck of USS *Yorktown* Photographer 2nd Class William G. Roy. The angular structure in the right foreground is the front of *Yorktown*'s forward starboard 5-inch gun gallery. The knotted lines hanging down from the carrier's flight deck are left over from the carrier's initial abandonment on 4 June. (USNHHC)

Above: The moment that USS *Hammann* finally slipped beneath the waves. The destroyer sank in just four minutes with the loss of some eighty men. (USNHHC)

Below: As the battle raged on, USS *Hornet*'s attack group returned to their carrier at 10.45 hours. Twenty-four of the Dauntlesses were refuelled and rearmed with 1,000lb bombs and, at 13.30 hours, took to the sky again. At

15.00 hours contact was made with the enemy ships again, the two cruisers and the destroyers *Arashio* and *Asashio* being still afloat. The Dauntlesses attacked.

Mogami was hit again amidships, the bomb penetrated the deck and killed men that were fighting the earlier fires. It also damaged the doors leading to the engine room, trapping men in the fire. More than ninety men were killed in this attack. *Mikuma* was also hit again a number of times and was rendered little more than a floating wreck. *Arashio* was also hit on her stern with a bomb, killing almost all the survivors from *Mikuma* who were on deck.

The fourth ship of the Japanese group was the destroyer *Asashio*. She suffered medium damage when she was hit by one 500lb bomb, which killed twenty-two crewmen. She assisted *Arashio* in rescuing 240 survivors from *Mikuma* then escorted the crippled *Mogami* to Truk on 14 June.

By the artist Robert Benny, and dated 1943, this somewhat imaginative painting depicts 'a withering attack upon a Japanese cruiser by Navy dive-bombers with a fighter escort'. (USNHHC)

Above: Another view of the battered *Mikuma* photographed from a Dauntless from the USS *Enterprise*.

Note her shattered midships structure, torpedo dangling from the after port side tubes and wreckage atop her number four eight-inch gun turret. Aircraft from *Enterprise* reported *Mikuma* still afloat at 17.30 hours. (USNHHC)

Right: Of the bombs that struck *Mikuma*, one hit the cruiser amidships and set off several of its Type 93 torpedoes. The resulting explosions destroyed the ship and severely wounded Captain Sakiyama.

Mikuma rolled to port and sank during the night, taking 650 men with it to the bottom. Captain Sakiyama was amongst those who

were rescued by *Asashio*. He was transferred to *Suzuya* for medical attention, but he died four days later. (USNHHC)

Above: This drawing, completed in 1942, depicts the heavy cruiser *Mikuma* capsizing to port and sinking.

The attacks on the two cruisers had, unwittingly, brought Spruance's carriers close to Yamamoto's main force. Even at this late stage of the battle and with his carriers wrecked, the Japanese commander still hoped to draw the Americans onto the guns of his powerful battleships and the great victory he had envisaged would be his. But his original plan had seen the three groups into which he had divided his force far too widely spread for him to bring them together in any realistic timescale, plus his ships were, by this time, low on fuel. Yamamoto had no choice but to accept the defeat of his plan and head his ships back home. (USNHHC)

Chapter 8
THE END OF USS YORKTOWN
7 June 1942

Above: After the attack by *I-168* on 6 June, USS *Vireo* took the salvage crew off *Yorktown* and all the water-tight doors that remained undamaged were closed. As dawn broke over the Pacific, the carrier remained stubbornly afloat; but by 05.30 hours on 7 June, observers noted that her list was rapidly increasing to port. At 07.01 hours, before the salvage party could be put back on board, *Yorktown* turned over onto her port side, rolled upside-down, and sank, stern first, in 3,000 fathoms of water. Here the final dramatic moments of *Yorktown* have been captured by a crewman from an accompanying destroyer. This view looking aft has the carrier's forefoot in the centre foreground and the forward end of her flight deck in the right centre. Note the froth caused by air escaping from the hull. (USNHHC)

Above: Another photograph of *Yorktown* as she capsized to port, with her bow nearest to the camera. This view looks toward the ship's bottom from off her bow, with *Yorktown*'s forefoot in the right foreground and her starboard forward five-inch gun gallery beyond. The large hole made by one or two submarine torpedoes, severing the ship's forward bilge keel, is towards the left. The

destroyer USS *Monaghan* is in the background. (USNHHC)

Below: In this view of the wreck of *Yorktown* the large hole made by one or two of *I-168*'s torpedoes can again be seen in the centre. *Yorktown*'s starboard forward 5-inch gun gallery is in the left centre, with two 5"/38 gun barrels sticking out over its edge. The two

larger thin objects sticking up, just aft of the 5-inch guns, are aircraft parking outriggers. When the carrier's wreck was examined in May 1998, both guns were still in position, but the outriggers were gone. (USNHHC)

Above: In this view of the sinking upturned *Yorktown*, the forward starboard corner of her flight deck is visible near the sea surface at the extreme right, with the bow Landing Signal Officer's platform extending upward from it. (USNHHC)

Below: One of the last pictures of USS *Yorktown* as the carrier settles rapidly by the stern, with the speed of her motion perhaps causing the moderate fuzziness of this image. (USNHHC)

A total of 141 officers and men from *Yorktown* lost their lives during the Battle of Midway. In this photograph, the cruiser USS *Portland* (on the right), transfers *Yorktown* survivors to USS *Fulton* on 7 June 1942. (USNHHC)

Chapter 9

AFTER THE BATTLE

The submarine tender USS *Fulton* arriving at Pearl Harbor in the early hours of 8 June with survivors from *Yorktown* on board. Among the tugs assisting Fulton are *Hoga* and *Nokomis*. The only two American ships lost during the Battle of Midway were *Yorktown* and *Hammann*. (USNHHC)

Above: *Yorktown* survivors board trucks for transportation to Camp Catlin, Oahu, soon after their arrival at Pearl Harbor on board USS *Fulton*, 8 June 1942. (USNHHC)

Opposite page top: Amongst those on the dock at Pearl Harbor watching USS *Fulton* arrive were Rear Admiral William L. Calhoun (in the right centre, wearing sunglasses) and Rear Admiral Lloyd J. Wiltse (in the centre background), of Admiral Nimitz's staff. (USNHHC)

Opposite page bottom: Survivors of USS *Hammann* are seen here being taken ashore at Pearl Harbor from USS *Benham*, a few days after their ship was sunk. (NARA)

The submarine USS *Trout* returns to Pearl Harbor on 14 June 1942. She is carrying two Japanese prisoners of war, Chief Radioman Hatsuichi Yoshida and Fireman 3rd Class Kenichi Ishikawa, survivors of the sunken cruiser *Mikuma* who had been rescued on 9 June. Among those waiting on the pier are Rear Admiral Robert H. English and Admiral Nimitz. (USNHHC)

Opposite page top: Japanese prisoners of war, survivors of the aircraft carrier *Hiryu*, are brought ashore at Midway following their rescue from an open lifeboat by USS *Ballard* on 19 June 1942. After being held for a few days on Midway, they were sent on to Pearl Harbor on 23 June. Note the US Marines guards at left and in the centre background. (USNHHC)

Opposite page below: Rewarding the victors. A shipboard awards ceremony was held at Pearl Harbor on 17 June to reward those who had inflicted the heaviest defeat upon the Japanese Imperial Navy since the war began.

Left to right the officers are: Vice Admiral William L. Calhoun, Commander, Service Force

Pacific Fleet; Rear Admiral Frank Jack Fletcher, Commander, Task Force 17; Rear Admiral Thomas C. Kinkaid, Commander, Cruiser Division 6; Rear Admiral William Ward Smith, Commander, Task Group 17.2; Rear Admiral Marc A. Mitscher; and Rear Admiral Robert H. English, Commander, Submarines Pacific Fleet. (USNHHC)

Above: After the battle, Admiral Nimitz, Commander in Chief, United States Pacific Fleet, went to Midway to inspect the damage caused by the Japanese attack. Here, the admiral inspects the damage done by the Japanese air attack on Sand and Eastern Islands of the Midway Group. (USNHHC)

Above: Admiral Nimitz is shown here exiting a bunker during his post-battle trip to Midway. (USNHHC)

Opposite page: During Nimitz's visit to Midway an officer explained how the Japanese air attack unfolded to the admiral. (USNHHC)

Right: A photograph was taken of Admiral Nimitz on board a barge which took him between Sand Island and Eastern Island. (USNHHC)

Above: One of the main reasons for Admiral Nimitz's visit to Midway was to decorate many of those who had helped defend the island during the battle, and here he can be seen presenting medals to Navy and Marine Corps personnel. (USNHHC)

Opposite page top: A cutter from the sunken Japanese aircraft carrier *Hiryu* is pictured here suspended from the starboard boat davits of USS *Ballard* at Midway in late June. This boat had been picked up on 19 June, along with its occupants, who became prisoners of war. (USNHHC)

Opposite page bottom: Japanese prisoners of war on board USS *Ballard* after being rescued from a lifeboat two weeks after the Battle of Midway.

They were members of the aircraft carrier *Hiryu*'s engineering force, left behind when she was abandoned on 5 June 1942, and had escaped in one of her boats just as she sank. (USNHHC)

Above: Those Japanese sailors from *Hiryu* who had been rescued by USS *Ballard* are shown here at Midway. After being held for a few days on Midway, they were sent on to Pearl Harbor on 23 June aboard USS *Sirius*, arriving there on 1 July. Only thirty-seven Japanese were taken prisoner, with 3,057 being killed. The greatest loss to the Japanese Imperial Navy was its carrier pilots, almost all of whom involved in the battle were killed. All the carrier-borne aircraft – 248 in total – were destroyed, and all four Japanese carriers were sunk as well as the cruiser *Mikuma*. (USNHHC)

Opposite top: A Japanese prisoner of war, one of the survivors of the aircraft carrier *Hiryu* who had been rescued by USS *Ballard*, reading the 24 November 1941 issue of *Life* magazine while being held on Midway pending transfer to Hawaii, circa 20-23 June 1942. (USNHHC)

Opposite bottom: Survivors from the aircraft carrier *Hiryu* are prepared for transportation from Midway to Hawaii on USS *Sirius*, 23 June 1942.

They had been rescued by USS *Ballard* a few days earlier. (USNHHC)

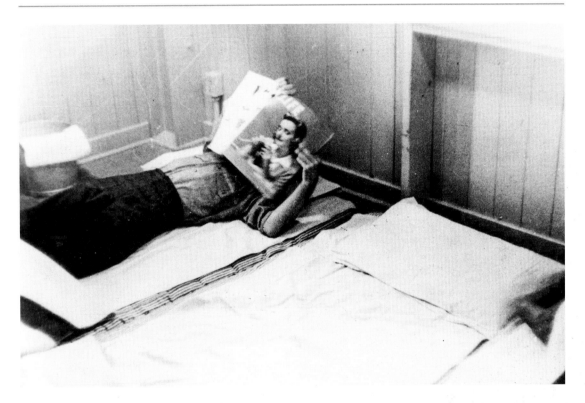

The USS *Pensacola* alongside Sand Island pier, Midway, disembarking US Marine reinforcements, 25 June 1942. The aircraft in the foreground, with a damaged tail, is the TBF-1 with the Bureau Number 00380, the only survivor of the VT-8 Avengers that attacked the Japanese fleet on 4 June 1942. The warship in the right distance is probably USS *Ballard*. (USNHHC)

Left: Another view of USS *Pensacola* disembarking US Marine reinforcements at the Sand Island pier, Midway, on 25 June 1942. The Sand Island seaplane hangar, which was badly damaged by Japanese air attack on 4 June 1942, is in the left distance, with a water tower beside it.

The surviving VT-8) TBF-1 Avenger, Bureau Number 00380, can just be seen on the beach, in line with the water tower. (USNHHC)

Above: A photograph of Aviation Radioman 3rd Class Douglas M. Cossitt (right) and Aviation Radioman 1st Class W.A. Miller at Naval Air Station, Alameda, California, on 4 September 1942.

The two men, at the time of the battle assigned to Torpedo Squadron Six from USS *Enterprise*, spent seventeen days in a life raft after their TBD-1 torpedo plane ditched on 4 June 1942.

The plane's pilot was Machinist Albert W. Winchell. Recovered by a Catalina on 21 June, some 360 miles north of Midway, they were the last of the downed Battle of Midway American aviators to be rescued. ARM1c Miller was also a survivor of the Battle of Coral Sea. (NARA)

MIDWAY

THE UNITED STATES OF AMERICA
HONORS THE COURAGE, SACRIFICE AND
ACHIEVEMENTS OF THE AMERICAN ARMED
FORCES WHO SUCCESSFULLY DEFENDED
THIS ISLAND AND ITS SURROUNDING SEAS
AGAINST THE EMPIRE OF JAPAN DURING
THE PERIOD 4-7 JUNE 1942.
OUTNUMBERED AND OUTGUNNED, THEY
WITHSTOOD SAVAGE BOMBARDMENT, FOUGHT
BACK, AND CARRIED THE FIGHT TO THE ENEMY.
DARING AIR STRIKES IN THE FACE OF
FIERCE RESISTANCE SANK FOUR ENEMY
AIRCRAFT CARRIERS, TURNING THE TIDE
OF WORLD WAR II IN THE PACIFIC.
AFTER THIS BATTLE OF MIDWAY THE UNITED
STATES AND ITS ALLIES FORGED AHEAD WITH
EVER INCREASING STRENGTH AND CONFIDENCE
TO FINAL VICTORY, SECURING THE BLESSINGS
OF FREEDOM AND LIBERTY FOR GENERATIONS
YET UNBORN.

Opposite: The Midway Monument is located on Midway Atoll at the north-western portion of the Hawaiian island chain. Erected in August 2015, the memorial is managed by the American Battle Monuments Commission. The inscription reads:

'The United States of America honors the courage, sacrifice, and achievements of the American armed forces who successfully defended this island and its surrounding seas against the Empire of Japan during the period of 4-7 June 1942. Outnumbered and outgunned, they withstood savage bombardment, fought back, and carried the fight to the enemy. Daring air strikes in the face of fierce resistance sank four enemy aircraft carriers, turning the tide of World War II in the Pacific. After the Battle of Midway, the United States and its Allies forged ahead with ever increasing strength and confidence to final victory, securing the blessings of freedom and liberty for generations yet unborn.'

Indeed, after the Battle of Midway, the Japanese carrier force which had wrecked the battleships of the Pacific Fleet at Pearl Harbor was no more, its planes, its men and its ships had gone. Following the events of 7 December 1941, the destruction of so many US ships had left the Japanese with the largest naval force in the Pacific, but that advantage had been blown away in just a few devastating minutes on 4 June 1942.

The Battle of Midway was the first major American naval victory over the Japanese and has, quite justifiably, been called the turning point in the war in the Pacific. It gave Admiral Nimitz the freedom to mount operations against Japanese-held territory, the first demonstration of this being the Guadalcanal campaign, the first important Allied offensive in the Pacific theatre, which began on 7 August 1942, just two months after Midway.

Though there was much fighting, dreadful, brutal fighting, to be done, the Japanese ship building capacity and their training organisation were too limited to enable them to make good their losses. Of the Battle of Midway, there was one inescapable conclusion: Midway was probably the best chance for Japan to destroy US naval power in the Pacific before America's enormous war industry created another new fleet entirely.

Just months after Midway, new American Essex-class carriers – the most lethal afloat – would be launched. Before the war ended, seventeen of the planned twenty-four carriers would see action.

In contrast, Japan launched only four more fleet carriers to replace its growing losses. Japanese naval aircraft – the best in the world in 1941 – were becoming obsolete by mid-1942. Furthermore, in the months after Midway, tens of thousands of new and superior Hellcat fighters, Avenger torpedo bombers and Helldiver dive bombers rolled off American assembly lines in numbers unmatched by the Japanese.

After 4 June 1942 there could only be one outcome to the Pacific War – the defeat of Imperial Japan. (American Battle Monuments Commission)

REFERENCES AND NOTES

1. Japan Defence Agency Historical Division, Tokyo, War History Publications Series, Vol.43, *The Midway Operations, May-June 1942*, (Tokyo, 1971), p.87, quoted in Peter C. Smith, *Dauntless Victory: Fresh Perspectives on America's Seminal Naval Victory of World War II* (Pen & Sword, Barnsley, 2007), p.5.
2. Robert O'Neil (Ed.), *The Pacific War: From Pearl Harbor to Okinowa* (Osprey, Oxford, 2015), p.67.
3. Edwin T. Layton, Roger Pineau, and John Costello, *And I Was There, Pearl Harbor and Midway – Breaking the Secrets* (William Morrow and Company, New York, 1985), p.422.
4. James D'Angelo, *Victory at Midway: The Battle That Changed the Course of World War II* (McFarland & Co, Jefferson, 2018), p.68.
5. ibid.
6. See E.B. Potter, *The Great Sea War: The Story of Naval Action in World War II* (Verdun Press, 2015).
7. Quoted on www.padresteve.com.
8. Information provided by the Missing Marines project, see www.missingmarines.com.
9. Quoted from the website of the US National Naval Aviation Museum: www.navalaviationmuseum.org.
10. ibid.
11. Harry H. Ferrier, 'Torpedo 8: The other Chapter', *Naval History Magazine*, June 2008, vol.22, No.3.
12. Bureau of Naval Personnel Information Bulletin No.312, March 1943.
13. Lieutenant Colonel R.D. Heinl, Jr., *Marines at Midway*, a Historical Monograph by the USMC Historical Section, Division of Public Information, (US Marine Corps Headquarters, 1948), p.35.
14. ibid.
15. The National Archives (TNA), AIR 23/4706.
16. Mitsuo Fuchiada and Masatake Okumiya, *Midway: The Battle That Doomed Japan* (Hutchinson, London, 1957), p.174.
17. US Navy Action Reports, The Battle of Midway, in the archives of the US Naval History and Heritage Command.
18. For more information, see: www.pacificwar.org.au
19. Quoted from www.cv6.org/site/association.htm.
20. Peter C. Smith, p.143.
21. Fuchiada and Okumiya, pp.180-1.
22. *The Battle of Midway* (Publication Section, Combat Intelligence Branch, US Navy, Washington D.C., 1943).
23. ibid, p.31.
24. ibid.
25. TNA, AIR 23/4706.
26. Fuchida and Okumiya, p.223.
27. C.C. Hartigan, Battle of Midway: 4-7 June 1942, Online Action Reports: Commanding Officer, USS *Hammann* (DD-412), Serial 2 of 16 June 1942.